Mar.

I'll ...... you

forever (quote)

Philip

Challenging behaviour and autism

Making sense – making progress

A guide to preventing and managing challenging behaviour for parents and teachers

Philip Whitaker

With contributions from
Helen Joy
Jane Harley
David Edwards

© The National Autistic Society

Acknowledgements

First and foremost, thanks are due to all the children with autistic spectrum disorders, parents and school staff with whom I have worked. The strategies that they have shared and helped develop (and some of the lessons learned from the inevitable failures) are the basis of the approaches described in this book. All the examples and anecdotes are based on real situations, although details have been changed to preserve anonymity.

I owe a great debt of gratitude to Helen Joy for her continual encouragement, her constructive suggestions and her willingness to share her considerable practical experience. Thanks also to Jane Harley and David Edwards for the strategies they contributed, and to Jenny Ravenhill and Barbara Dewar for their extremely constructive reviews and helpful suggestions.

Finally, a word of thanks to my children, Emily and Jo, who gave up many an assignation with Lara Croft so that I could use the computer.

About the author and contributors

Philip Whitaker is an educational psychologist with specialist responsibility for autism working in Leicestershire's Educational Psychology Service.

Helen Joy, at the time of writing, was the Professional Leader of Leicestershire's Autism Outreach Team. She is now Senior Teacher at Forest Way School, Coalville, Leicestershire.

Jane Harley and **David Edwards** work as members of Leicestershire's Autism Outreach Team.

First published 2001 by The National Autistic Society, 393 City Road, London EC1V 1NG
Reprinted 2003 and 2005

All rights reserved. No part of this publication may be reproduced, stored in a retrieval system or transmitted, in any form or by any means, electronic, mechanical, photocopying, recording or otherwise without the prior permission of the Copyright owner.

ISBN 1 899280 51 0

Copyright © The National Autistic Society

Designed by Cottier and Sidaway

Printed in Great Britain by Stephen Austin & Sons Ltd

Contents

Introduction

Who is this book for?

This book is written for parents, carers and staff working in educational settings – indeed, anyone who is involved in looking after or educating a youngster who experiences some form of autistic spectrum disorder – whether this has been described as autism, Asperger syndrome, or any of the other 'labels' currently in use. The focus is on *practical* strategies for preventing and managing challenging behaviour, most of which can be used equally well at home and at school. We have highlighted the sorts of problems that are likely to occur in both settings, and have included difficulties that can occur right across the autistic spectrum.

Throughout the book we have made as few assumptions as possible about your background knowledge. Though we hope the book will be of interest to those who do have more specialised, in-depth knowledge of autism or behaviour management, we have tried to avoid taking this sort of background knowledge for granted.

What are the aims of the book?

Four main aims have guided the writing of this book.

- **Putting the emphasis on prevention** Children with autistic spectrum disorders may be more likely than other children to develop challenging behaviour. However, careful management can help to prevent problems or reduce the likelihood of patterns of challenging behaviour becoming entrenched.
- **Helping make sense of challenging behaviour** This is a theme that is returned to again and again. Understanding the meaning of a child's behaviour – what purpose it serves for him or her puts us in a much better position to do something about it.
- **Offering examples of practical solutions** When parents and teachers discuss the behaviour of children with autistic spectrum disorders, a range of problems crop up repeatedly. Throughout the book we draw on the experiences of parents and teachers to illustrate the ways in which some of these problems have been successfully tackled.
- **Providing a framework for solving problems** As well as making use of other people's experience, you need a framework that helps you think through the particular problems and situations you are facing in a systematic way. The framework provided here should enable you to make sense of the problem, then help generate ideas for tackling it, building on your understanding of what lies behind the behaviour.

How to use this book

If you have already looked at the Contents, you will have noticed that the book is not divided into chapters dealing with particular types of problems. This is because the answer to the question 'What do you do about such and such a behaviour?' almost always starts with the words 'That depends ...' It will depend on the child's strengths and difficulties. It will depend on when, where and how often the behaviour occurs. Above all, it will depend on what the behaviour is about – the motivation that drives it and the purposes it serves for a particular child.

Because other people's solutions will not always fit your problems, the first section of the book provides you with a framework that helps you to make sense of *your* child's behaviour. The framework then guides you through a series of steps that help you systematically work out strategies for preventing or dealing with the difficulties. Each section of the book focuses on a different part of the framework and each section provides a wide range of practical suggestions linked to that step in the framework.

Each chapter includes pen pictures and anecdotes illustrating how particular approaches or strategies have been applied in real-life situations. For some of the problems that most frequently cause concern, we have drawn on our experience to offer guidelines and tips. The index allows you to find the descriptions, case studies, anecdotes and guidelines that are relevant to the behaviour that you are most concerned about.

A word about words

Throughout the book we have attempted to keep jargon and specialised vocabulary to a minimum (providing explanations where this has been unavoidable). However, there are a few words and phrases used throughout the book that need some comment.

- **Challenging behaviour** This is one piece of jargon that we have made a conscious decision to use, though we recognise that the majority of parents will have other, much more direct (and possibly colourful) ways of referring to their child's behaviour. We prefer this term because it seems to deal with the problem of definition and captures the essence of all the many different forms of behaviour that we refer to throughout the book. In a nutshell, 'challenging behaviour' is behaviour that challenges – whether it is a challenge to our understanding, our own well-being or our child's or else to our ability to carry out our responsibilities as parents or professionals.
- **Children with autistic spectrum disorders** Rather than referring specifically to 'autism' or to 'Asperger syndrome' (or any of the other more specific diagnostic labels that are in use), we prefer to use the broader term 'autistic spectrum disorder'. This term includes any youngster who has a degree of difficulty in each of the three core areas of development necessary for diagnosis of autism to be made (see beginning of Chapter 1).
- **Your child** We use this phrase to refer to the child you have responsibility for, whether this is in your capacity as a parent, carer or a member of staff in a school or other educational setting.
- **He** We have chosen to refer to all children as if they were male. This reflects the fact that there are many more boys with autistic spectrum disorders than there are girls. However, our main reason for doing this is to avoid the repetitive use of 'he or she' and 'him or her'. We hope that this does not cause offence and, as our case studies and so on show, we recognise that girls with autistic spectrum disorders can be every bit as challenging as boys who have them.

1
Autism and challenging behaviour – understanding the link

Introduction

Children with autistic spectrum disorders have problems in three main areas of their development (usually referred to as the 'triad of impairments'):

- social interaction and understanding
- all aspects of communication – verbal and non-verbal
- flexibility of thinking and behaviour, including problems with imagination.

The severity of each of these difficulties will vary quite considerably from child to child. There will also be a good deal of variation in the ways the difficulties show themselves and how they affect day-to-day coping. Each child will have his own profile of skills and abilities and his own unique personality. We now know that autistic spectrum disorders have a biological cause. However, it is also important to emphasise that the picture each child presents will be influenced by learning and experience.

At the very outset, it is very important to stress that there is no inevitable link between autistic spectrum disorders and challenging behaviour. When a child has some form of autism, this does not mean that he will necessarily go on to develop behaviour difficulties. Just as importantly, if your child is presenting challenging behaviour at the moment, this does not mean that it will be a feature throughout his life. Skills and coping strategies develop – both your child's and your own.

Having said this, there is no doubt that challenging behaviour is a good deal more common in children with autistic spectrum disorders. Their particular difficulties increase their vulnerability to developing behaviour that presents a significant challenge to carers and teachers. Once these patterns become established, they can be very resistant to change. Everyday methods that most adults successfully use to influence and shape other children's behaviour may not be effective.

This book is intended to help you prevent patterns of challenging behaviour from becoming established and offer practical strategies and tips for dealing with specific problems if they do arise. Throughout the book we come back, again and again, to a central theme:

To change your child's behaviour you need to be able to make sense of that behaviour, and making sense of your child's behaviour means making sense of his autism.

In the rest of this chapter, we look in turn at each of the core impairments that underlie autism and the ways in which these may affect your child's behaviour.

Problems of social interaction – relating to others

For many years, the classic, and commonest, image of autism was of a child who showed no interest in (or actually avoided) contact and interaction with others. As understanding of autistic spectrum disorders has increased, a broader and more varied picture of social difficulties has been recognised. Some children do seem to be indifferent to other people, may seem to 'live in world of their own' and may be distressed by efforts to interact with them. They may make use of other people to ensure their needs are met, but this has a rather impersonal feel. Parents often say that 'it feels as if you are being used as a tool'. Another group of children appear to make no active effort to initiate interaction, but they may respond if others take the initiative. A pattern observed in a third group of children resulted in Lorna Wing's description 'active but odd'. These are the children who may be very interested in social contact with others, but who tend to break the 'unwritten rules' as to how to go about this. They may talk at others, rather than with them, can appear rather intrusive and may be inappropriately familiar or too formal and rather stilted.

There has been a great deal of debate about the exact nature of these social difficulties. A lot of work has focused on trying to decide whether or not these problems have a main underlying cause. Though research continues, there is now a fair measure of agreement that a central difficulty for people with autistic spectrum disorders is what one writer has termed 'mindblindness'. This is a shorthand way of capturing their difficulty in instinctively sensing, caring about and understanding other people's feelings, beliefs and intentions, which seems to be such a conspicuous feature of autism. (Anyone interested in a more detailed discussion of this topic is recommended to read the book by Francesca Happé, listed in the Further Reading section.)

In the table overleaf we spell out some of the problems that such underlying difficulties can create. It is relatively easy to imagine how these behaviours could be seen as challenging in themselves or else how they could easily create a situation where challenging behaviour is the result. The problem is not only one of your child misunderstanding other people, but of them misunderstanding him. If they interpret his behaviour as cheek or defiance, then their reactions are likely to make matters worse.

An underlying difficulty in ...	creates a problem with ...
enjoying contact with people (or actively disliking it)	■ being frightened or stressed by contact with other people ■ reducing the motivation to communicate ■ restricting opportunities (and motivation) to learn from, and about, other people ■ not being bothered about pleasing other people (so not doing as they are asked)
understanding other people's feelings	■ causing offence without being aware ■ forming and keeping friendships or other close relationships ■ knowing how to react to other people's feelings ■ appearing egocentric or insensitive
understanding other people's reactions	■ making sense of unspoken messages about how to behave in certain situations ■ understanding other people's intentions ■ being able to get at the message behind people's words
making sense of the rules in social situations	■ knowing how and when to join in ■ appearing too familiar or pushy ■ coming over as too formal or standoffish ■ going too far without realising

Communication

There is an enormously wide variation in the range of communication skills and strategies acquired by children with autistic spectrum disorders. Quite a large minority (as many as one in four or five) may never develop speech or get past the stage of echoing words and phrases that they have heard others using. Even when speech and language seems to develop along normal lines, a youngster is likely to have subtle, but significant, difficulties in using language in social situations and for social purposes. These problems may be most obvious when someone tries to involve them in a 'to and fro' conversation.

Unfortunately, these difficulties do not only affect spoken forms of communication. Children with autistic spectrum disorders also have problems with what are usually termed the 'non-verbal' aspects of communication. They may have difficulty in learning to use pointing and gesture, which could otherwise be used to compensate for difficulties with spoken language. Problems also occur with the more subtle forms of non-verbal communication – for instance, using eye contact as a way of making a connection before communicating or to show that you are expecting the other person to reply.

All children with autistic spectrum disorders also have some degree of difficulty in understanding the communication of others. Some children seem to take a long time to learn that 'things have names' or that speech is a special sort of 'noise', different from all the other sounds in their environment. They may have difficulty grasping the skill of following the direction of someone else's gaze and sharing a focus of attention with that person, having no clue what the adult's words are referring to. Even when quite sophisticated levels of understanding have been achieved, a person with an autistic spectrum disorder may have problems in going beyond the meaning of individual words and sentences to get at the speaker's intentions and feelings. Abstract concepts and 'turns of phrase' (expressions such as 'stretch your legs', usually referred to as 'non-literal speech') may present particular stumbling blocks. Although the child may understand the individual sentences in a long instruction or explanation, he may have difficulties putting them together to grasp the main ideas behind what is being said.

An underlying difficulty in ...	creates a problem with ...
expressing needs	■ letting someone know what he wants (or even that he does want something) ■ asking for help ■ explaining that he is worried or in pain ■ explaining that he does not understand ■ showing what he does not want
using language in social situations	■ letting people know that he has got something to tell them ■ keeping a conversation going ■ making sure that the other person gets a turn in the conversation ■ knowing if the other person understands or is interested
understanding other people's language and communication	■ understanding what other people want him to do ■ understanding what other people do not want him to do ■ making sense of why they want him to do those things ■ interpreting what others are 'saying' with their bodies, faces and tone of voice
taking things literally	■ how to tell if someone really means what they are saying or if it is just a 'turn of phrase' ■ how to avoid looking silly

The communication problems experienced by children with autistic spectrum disorders contribute directly to many of the challenging behaviours they can present. The table on the previous page highlights some of the underlying difficulties in communication and the problems these can create for your child.

Flexibility of thinking and behaviour

There is some disagreement about just how to describe and sum up the core features of this third area of the triad. It is sometimes referred to as an impairment of imagination, but the problems seem to extend beyond this, to a broader difficulty in thinking and behaving with flexibility and creativity. As with the other two areas of the triad, there is a great deal of variability in the form these difficulties take and in the extent to which they affect the child's (and the family's) day-to-day life. The extent of any additional learning difficulties seems to have a very important effect on how these problems are manifested.

Children who are very young or at a relatively early developmental level may become hooked on very specific physical sensations. They may be fascinated by looking at things from a particular angle or watching things that spin. Lights may fascinate them or they may be tuned in to other senses – particular textures, smells or sounds holding their attention. Sometimes a child creates the sensations by their own repetitive movements, such as spinning, flapping or tapping. The patterns of play that emerge at a later stage may be quite restricted. A child may only focus on one very specific feature of a toy or concentrate on making collections or arrangements of objects. If imaginative play does develop, this may be quite repetitive or inflexible – repeatedly acting out scenes from the same video or insisting that a game be always played in exactly the same way, for example. In older and more able children, these difficulties may take the form of intense interests or obsessions. Sometimes the focus of interest may seem rather peculiar – such as street lights, circuit diagrams or vacuum cleaners. Alternatively, it may be the strength of the fascination, and its domination of the child's life, that is unusual.

Problems of inflexibility are also apparent from the routines, rituals and resistance to change that are frequently a feature of autistic spectrum disorders. These have been very neatly summed up as a 'need for sameness'. Children may create rituals and routines for themselves – insisting that things are arranged, done or even said in a certain way. It is also common for them to latch on to the way things have been done (by a parent or teacher) and then insist that this is the way they should always be done in the future. Always wanting to go on the same route, to the same shops is an example that will be familiar to many parents, and resistance to unfamiliar foods is especially common.

In the past, these aspects of autistic spectrum disorders have been the subject of relatively little research and investigation. The reasons for them (and why they occur alongside the other two features of the triad) are still unclear. It seems reasonable to assume, however, that some of these behaviours develop as a response to the problems of communication and social interaction. Difficulties in making sense of other people and anticipating what is about to happen (which is one aspect of imagination) may result in high levels of anxiety. Rituals and routines may provide a way of reducing this anxiety, creating a sense of 'sameness'. Many of the highly focused interests or repetitive actions may be a way of blocking out the demands of coping with people.

Problems with flexibility are very closely linked to challenging behaviour. The repetitive behaviours, rituals and restricted interests may be challenging in themselves. More commonly, however, problems arise when the environment (and the people who are such a vital part of that environment) is unable to accommodate the youngster's 'need for sameness'. The following table illustrates some of these problems.

An underlying difficulty in ...	creates a problem with ...
needing 'sameness' and routine	<ul><li>dealing with unexpected and unavoidable changes to routines</li><li>making transitions from one activity to another</li><li>handling any sort of uncertainty about what is happening next or what will happen in the future</li><li>dealing with anxiety if the 'need for sameness' cannot be met</li></ul>
having repetitive patterns of play, rituals and obsessions	<ul><li>restricting opportunities for developing and learning other, more productive or appropriate skills</li><li>isolating your child from interaction with other people</li><li>intruding into, and restricting, the lives of other people in your child's environment</li></ul>
imagination	<ul><li>anticipating what might be going to happen in the future</li><li>predicting the consequences of actions</li><li>recognising danger</li></ul>

Learning and sensory difficulties

There are several other areas of difficulty that are quite commonly associated with autistic spectrum disorders, though they do not have to be present for a diagnosis to be made. These can have a bearing on challenging behaviour.

There is a significant link between autism and learning difficulties. It is usually suggested that between half and two thirds of all people with autism have a significant degree of learning difficulty. It is hard to separate the effects of learning difficulty from the impact of autism. However, the degree of learning difficulty seems to have an important effect on the way in which the autism is manifested in an individual. This is most obvious in terms of any special interests or obsessions. When a youngster has severe learning difficulties, repetitive behaviours and interests tend to be simpler. They are often focused on repeating a single movement (such as spinning) or a very specific sensation (such as tapping or scratching particular surfaces).

Learning difficulties also have a broader impact. They affect your child's ability to understand and cope with the demands that are made on him. They influence the ease and speed with which new skills are learned. Anything that makes it more difficult for the individual to communicate his needs, function independently or occupy himself constructively is likely to increase frustration or boredom. This, in turn, makes it more likely that your child will resort to challenging behaviour.

Many children with autistic spectrum disorders seem to have unusual responses and sensitivity to sound, sight or their other bodily senses. They may seem fascinated by very specific sights – gazing at bright lights or reflections is particularly common – or may be totally preoccupied by some aspect of what we would think of as background noise. Strong interests in particular textures or tastes may also occur. These fascinations can have an influence on behaviour in a number of ways. Your child may become almost obsessed with gaining access to the sensation, with all the problems that arise when any obsession is thwarted. Difficulties often result from the effect that these fascinations have on your child's ability to pay attention and focus on other aspects of their environment. His ability to understand instructions or expectations may be reduced or he may 'lose the plot' when engaged in an activity.

It is probably more common for this oversensitivity to be shown either as a strong fear or dislike of particular sounds or, less commonly, visual input. Your child may show an especially intense reaction to loud sounds, but these may be sounds that most of us would find intrusive or unpleasant (such as motorcycles or washing machines). Often these fears or sensitivities are very specific – a child may not have a problem with other loud noises, even though we might. More puzzlingly (and this is less easy to spot), some children develop a strong aversion to particular sounds that we might barely notice or else certainly do not regard as unduly intrusive or unpleasant. For instance, the sound of hand dryers in public toilets often seems to cause difficulties. A less focused form of sensory difficulty can also occur when your child becomes overloaded with the sheer amount of stimulation that they are getting through a particular sense (typically sounds). These forms of oversensitivity can have very direct and dramatic effects on your child's behaviour:

- intense reactions to the physical sensations and the fear that may result
- attempts to escape or avoid the source of the sensation, such as running away or covering his ears
- anxiety or fear resulting from your child anticipating that the sound or sight is about to occur
- sensory overload, which is when your child's response to the sight or sounds (or his fear and anticipation) reduce his ability to carry out other tasks, such as paying attention to instructions or following them through.

Focusing on your child

We hope that we have managed to give you some insight into the core difficulties that underlie autism – and into the problems that can arise as a result. We have highlighted some of the most common of these and particularly emphasised those that often contribute to challenging behaviour. As we have said before, however, there is a great deal of variation in the way in which the core impairments manifest themselves and in their severity. Just as importantly, each child will differ in terms of their other skills and difficulties, personality and temperament and the environment in which they live.

12

Faced with a particular type of challenging behaviour, we need to make sense of its significance and meaning for that individual child in his particular environment. We need an understanding of his autistic spectrum disorders and the ways in which these interact with the demands the whole environment makes on him.

In the next chapter, we outline a framework that will help you to make sense of your child's behaviour and plan strategies for preventing and tackling the behaviours that concern you most.

2
Making sense of your child and planning for change

The need for a framework

When you are faced with challenging behaviour, it can be very difficult to know where to start and in what direction to go. Advice in books or from professionals will be strongly influenced by the individual's theoretical perspectives (or frameworks). Doctors may well start from an assumption that behaviour problems reflect some sort of organic difficulty and so may look towards the use of medication. Many psychiatrists used to work on the assumption that the problems experienced and presented by children with autistic spectrum disorders had a lot to do with their relationships with their parents. This led them to offer 'therapy' to the child and to try to change relationships within the family. It should be stressed that this view of autism and its 'treatment' has largely been discredited, but it does highlight the way in which a specific theory about the causes of a problem will lead to particular approaches to dealing with it. In contrast, psychologists and teachers may be more inclined to think in terms of the child's learning experiences and the skills he may (or may not) have acquired.

Even if we do not adhere to any particular theory (with a capital 'T'), most of us start out with some sort of framework, beliefs or set of assumptions when we begin to think about our child's behaviour. Think about the following statements.

- 'He knows exactly what he's doing.'
- 'You've got to show him who's boss.'
- 'He's exactly like his dad.'
- 'Setting rules will just stifle his individuality.'
- 'He can't help it, he's got no way of saying what he wants.'

Of course, these are just caricatures, but each might lead to a quite different set of priorities and to quite different courses of action. The same is true for theories in the more formal sense. Our frameworks (or theories) have a very important impact on:

- the feelings and gut reactions that we have towards the behaviour
- the way we 'interpret' the behaviour – for instance, whether we see our child as doing it 'on purpose' or not
- what we see as the cause of the behaviour
- what we think can be done about it – and how
- whose responsibility we think it should be.

Generally, it is not a matter of thinking of a specific framework as being right or wrong. Medical factors and organic conditions undoubtedly do play a significant part in some forms of challenging behaviour. A child's experiences in early infancy may sometimes play a role in the extent or type of challenging behaviour that he later presents. The most important consideration for a parent or teacher has to be whether a particular framework is *useful* or not. Does it focus on factors that may be under your control or you may be able to influence? Does it give you guidance about how to get started and where to head next? Does it help prevent other problems becoming established?

We will go on to describe a framework that, in our experience, most parents and teachers find *is* practical. That is to say, it offers some help with the sorts of questions posed at the end of the previous paragraph. Its focus is on helping you to make sense of your child's behaviour and linking that understanding to a systematic framework for tackling the problem. Before going into detail about the framework, we need to spell out the key assumptions on which it is based.

Key assumptions

Our approach is based on three main assumptions.

- **There is a significant learned component in most forms of challenging behaviour and what has been learned may be 'unlearned'** For all the reasons outlined in the first chapter, your child's autistic spectrum disorders make him vulnerable to developing challenging behaviour. They also make his management much more demanding and complicated for you. However, autism does not make challenging behaviour inevitable. If it does develop, then the form it takes will be shaped, to a considerable degree, by learning, by the influence of the whole environment and by your child's other skills. Controlling and shaping all these influences is difficult, but some degree of influence is usually possible.

- **Challenging behaviour almost always means something** Your child may have a very definite purpose in mind when he engages in challenging behaviour. Alternatively, his behaviour may be telling you something about his reactions and feelings.
  - Past experience may have taught him that he can achieve a particular result or outcome (even though we may not always understand why that outcome is so rewarding for our child).
  - Sometimes your child may be reacting to particular emotions that have been triggered by something in the environment – he may not be consciously trying to communicate his feelings.
  - Occasionally the challenging behaviour may have become a very strong form of habit. Your child may have originally been frightened or excited by an experience. This reaction then gets hooked on some feature of the environment or routine and is then triggered because of the association.

- **Understanding the behaviour helps us to change it** If we know what feature of the environment our child is reacting to and why it is creating the difficulty, we may be able to do something about it. If we know what pay-off the child is trying to achieve, then we may be able to teach him a better way reach his goal. It may be possible to tempt him to behave differently so that he brings about a different, bigger, better or more acceptable pay-off.

These assumptions form the foundation of the framework that underlies the remainder of this book. Whatever new discoveries are made about the underlying causes of autistic spectrum disorders, we believe that these assumptions will continue to offer commonsense, practical guidance to parents and teachers struggling with challenging behaviour. Just as importantly, these assumptions lead to approaches that are compatible with, and protect, your child's dignity and rights.

Introducing the Eight-step Plan

The Eight-step Plan is based on what is usually termed the 'behavioural approach' to challenging behaviour. This was originally developed by psychologists and has continued to evolve over the last two to three decades. The approach emphasises the learned element in all forms of challenging behaviour and the role of the environment in maintaining that behaviour (with the word 'environment' being interpreted in its broadest sense, including the people in your child's life). Particular attention is paid to the factors that may be at work immediately before the problem occurs and the impact and effects that the behaviour creates.

John Clements and Eva Zarkowska describe one variant of this overall approach, which they neatly term the STAR model. Each letter of this title reminds us of one of the key elements that we need to focus on when trying to make sense of, and change, behaviour:

- the Setting in which the problem occurs
- the Triggers or events that seem to set the problem off
- the Action – what the child actually does
- the Results of the behaviour – the effects it has and what it seems to achieve
  for the child.

Careful thought and observation focused on each of these elements can help us identify factors and influences that we may be able to change and control to bring about an improvement in behaviour.

These same 'STAR' factors are at the heart of the framework provided in our Eight-step Plan. The Plan helps you to:

- organise your thoughts and observations systematically
- make sense of your child's behaviour in terms of what the behaviour achieves or communicates for him
- focus on prevention
- develop an action plan that builds systematically on your observations and thinking about the problem.

The Eight-step Plan:
an overview

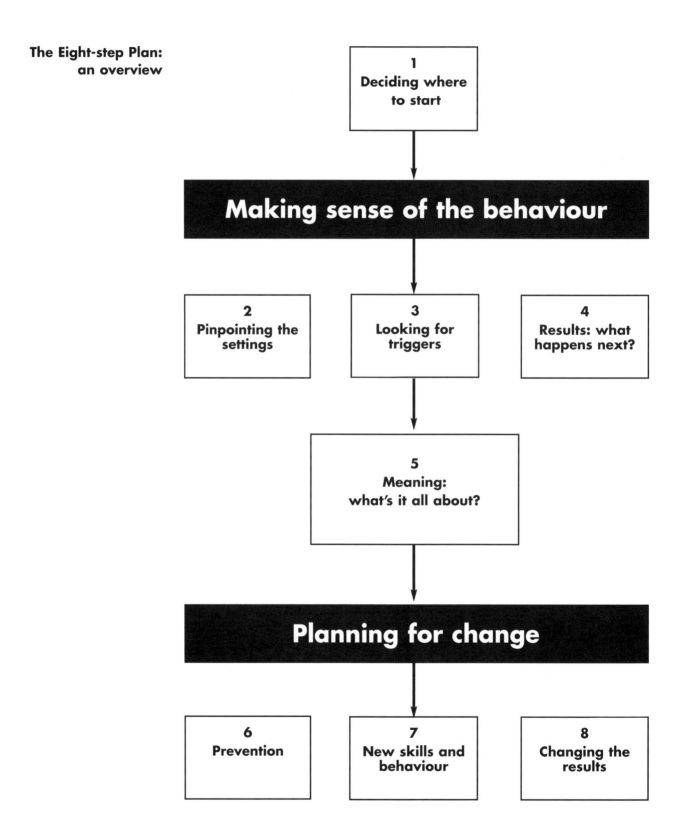

1
Deciding where
to start

Making sense of the behaviour

| **2** Pinpointing the settings | **3** Looking for triggers | **4** Results: what happens next? |

5
Meaning:
what's it all about?

Planning for change

| **6** Prevention | **7** New skills and behaviour | **8** Changing the results |

The Eight-step Plan

Below, each step of the plan is spelled out. In addition to explaining the overall focus of the steps, we identify the key questions that you need to ask and provide cross-references to other sections of the book that may be helpful in tackling them.

Before going any further, it must be stressed that we are not suggesting you use the plan for every difficulty you encounter in managing your child's behaviour. Some problems will not require such a sophisticated approach, and you may find that you gradually develop an instinct for ways of preventing or resolving difficulties. However, in our experience, when you are faced with a serious difficulty that does not seem to be responding to your usual strategies, working systematically through the Eight-step Plan can pay dividends. Perhaps not surprisingly, it is just when you are facing this sort of problem that your sense of urgency or anxiety means that it is most tempting to leap straight to a 'solution'. At these times, careful observation and systematic thought or discussion may seem to be a luxury that you cannot afford. Unfortunately, we have often found that these pressures have led us to overlook some important factor that is influencing the behaviour or our 'solution' has only addressed one component of the problem.

Making sense of the behaviour

The first four steps of the plan focus on helping you to make sense of what is happening and what might be the meaning or purpose of the behaviour.

Step 1: Deciding where to start

Unfortunately, problems do not always occur alone and usually you have to tackle one thing at a time. Occasionally, this seems to lead to more general improvements in areas of behaviour that you did not focus on, but, sadly, you cannot count on this. To help you decide where to start, do the following.

■ List the problem behaviours that concern you. Wherever possible, use 'doing' words – hitting, kicking, spitting and so on – rather than thinking in terms such 'being aggressive' or 'naughtiness'. Descriptions such as these tend to be quite vague, making it more difficult to focus your attempts to deal with the problem. They also make it more difficult to tell if there is any progress. Terms such as 'naughty' or 'disruptive' often imply something about the cause of the problem and about the child's motivation.
■ Try to weigh up the relative priorities of the different problems. For each problem, ask the following questions.
  ● Is it a danger to your child or to others?
  ● Does it interfere with his ability to learn?
  ● Does it restrict his access to important experiences?
  ● How much stress does it cause and for whom?
  ● How frequent is it, how intense and how long does it last?
■ Consider starting with one of the less serious problems so that you build up your confidence.

Once you have decided what you want to focus on, it can be helpful to keep a record for a couple of weeks. Depending on the problem, you may want to keep a count (per hour, per day, per week) or measure the duration of each incident. This will give you a baseline, so that you can tell if things are getting better or worse. As you observe and record, you may then want to focus on answering the questions in Steps 2, 3 and 4.

Case study

At the age of 11, it was difficult to know where to start with Mark. He had very few ways of keeping himself busy. Any toy or activity that he was given had a fair chance of being thrown to the floor (while Mark grinned and looked around). Once or twice a day he would suddenly charge across the room and give one of his parents or sisters a hefty slap. The same thing happened at school. A further problem was his habit of spitting – never at other people, but on to his T-shirt or the table immediately in front of him (usually followed by him 'drawing' in the spit). Though the slapping was the most obviously challenging behaviour, after some observation it was decided to focus on the spitting. This was because the spitting (and the smell that it led to) was putting people off having anything to do with Mark. Without people being really aware of it, the level of contact and interaction that they had with Mark was beginning to suffer. As Mark was actually quite motivated by contact with others, his quality of life was certainly suffering as opportunities to develop his social interaction and communication were being reduced.

Case study

Sally was always at the centre of some disturbance or other in her Year 4 class. She was always out of her seat on some pretext. While on her travels in the classroom, she would usually mess about with another child's bag or pencil box (these being some of her main interests). When the owner protested or tried to stop her, Sally usually reacted in a way that led to uproar (often hitting the other child or screaming that she hated him or her). Work with Sally and her teacher started by trying to reduce the number of times she left her seat in any one lesson. It was felt that this would reduce the scope for conflicts to arise. It was also recognised that attention would eventually need to be given to improving the quality of her relationships with her classmates (and reducing these conflicts was an important first step).

Step 2: Pinpointing the settings

The term 'setting' refers to all aspects of the environment in which the problem usually occurs. Building up a picture is generally a slow and gradual process. Finding the time to keep a diary or make a record (even if there are gaps) is extremely helpful. Comments and observations from other people who are not directly involved in coping with the situation can also be invaluable (but can be quite daunting to begin with). When you are thinking about the settings, make sure that you consider:

- when, where and with whom the problem occurs:
  - the levels of noise, crowding, heat, and so on
  - who else is nearby, doing what
  - how structured and predictable the situation is
- what your child *should* be doing in that situation
  - what the expectations are (and how clear they are)
  - whether or not they are reasonable and realistic
  - if your child understands them
  - whether he has the skills to cope with the expectations or not
- what your child's physical and emotional state is
- when the problem does *not* happen – the situations where the problem does not occur may give you important clues about settings and triggers, and how they might be avoided.

Daniel was a relatively able 12-year-old attending a very structured, specialist unit for youngsters with Asperger syndrome. The school staff experienced no major difficulties with him, but almost every night he would arrive home and almost immediately start to provoke his mum and his much younger sisters. The trigger often seemed to be his mum's attempt to find out what sort of a day he had had (reasonably, she assumed that, if there had been a difficulty, it would help Daniel to have a chance to get it off his chest). The problem may have been due to a build-up of tension during the day or because of the contrast between the structured school day and normal family life (or probably a combination of the two). Daniel responded well to a two-pronged strategy. He was encouraged to plan his evening activities using a simple timetable that included fixed points such as teatime, bedtime and so on. The after-school routine also included guaranteed 'down time' as soon as he got home – half an hour in his room, on his PlayStation, on his own.

Step 3: Looking for triggers

Triggers are the aspects of the environment and the situation that seem to spark off the problem. It may be that your child is just reacting. He sees something that frightens him, is overwhelmed by the demand that is being made or there is some association with an unpleasant experience in the past. Triggers may also work like signals to your child. He has learned that when he behaves in a certain way, in a particular situation, he will achieve a certain result. You may need to look very closely to spot the trigger and your child will not always respond to it. He may have good days when he is less anxious or feeling more confident about the situation, but even then the reaction will occur, if in a more muted form. Think about the following questions.

- Does someone make a particular demand?
- Does something make a particular demand?
- Is the trigger something that your child suddenly notices or pays attention to (even though nothing in the situation seems to have changed)?
- Could the trigger be something that does not happen when your child expects it to?
- Again, think about exceptions to the rule – are there times when the particular trigger does not have its usual effect?

Your answers – to this last question especially – may give you important clues about influences at work in the setting.

Quite out of the blue, Lisa's behaviour became very difficult to manage. She would drop to her knees and refuse to proceed, becoming very cross or agitated if an adult tried to get her to stand and walk on. The overwhelming impression was that she was frightened, rather than being awkward, but she did not have the communication skills to explain what the matter was. Putting together observations from home and school, it appeared that the problem was centred on particular places, rather than activities. Certain rooms in the school and certain shops that she had previously visited quite happily now seemed to be causing her real anxiety. To make matters worse, this anxiety seemed to be spilling over into other parts of Lisa's life. For example, not only would she not go inside the supermarket, but she began to get agitated if she had to walk down the street where it was. By a combination of careful observation and luck when they visited an unfamiliar shop, Lisa's father discovered that she had developed an intense fear of fans. It was never possible to work out what had triggered this fear in the first place, but the problem was reduced by means of a combination of strategies. Her level of fear was gradually reduced (though never eliminated) through desensitisation. Her parents and staff at school also made use of a specially prepared symbol showing a picture of a fan with a red cross through it. This was used to reassure Lisa that there were no fans in the particular environment that she was entering.

Step 4: Results – what happens next?

Think about the events that follow your child's actions or behaviour. Severe challenging behaviour may well set off a whole chain of events, with lots of things happening at once. Does your child seem to anticipate or be interested in or be rewarded by a particular result or consequence that follows his actions? You may need to look out for a pattern that emerges over time. Keep these possibilities in mind:

- your child could just be interested in making something happen (regardless of what that something is – just a wish to make a splash)
- the behaviour may create some physical or sensory results
- the reactions of other people – immediately after the behaviour, or some time later – may be rewarding to your child
- something might stop happening after the behaviour – such as people reducing their demands.

Case study

Carl attended a school for children with severe learning difficulties and was part of a very busy class containing a number of very demanding and noisy youngsters. He would often react to the noise by either putting his fingers in his ears or producing loud, repetitive sounds. On one occasion, he seemed especially distressed and hit out at a child in a wheelchair. Concern for Carl's obvious distress and for the other child's well-being led the teacher to make use of time out. With a classroom assistant supervising, Carl was put outside the classroom on a chair for five minutes. He returned to the classroom in a much better frame of mind. However, over the following weeks, aggression towards other children became increasingly common. His teacher eventually realised that she had inadvertently taught Carl a very effective way of escaping from a situation that was causing him distress. It proved difficult to deal with the source of the problem, but staff kept a closer eye on Carl and provided him with a form of time out whenever he seemed to be getting agitated, but before he resorted to aggression. His teacher also began to work on his ability to take the initiative for himself by providing him with a picture card that he could use to request time out.

Step 5: Meaning – what's it all about?

This is the point where you take stock. Your aim is to try and make sense of the challenging behaviour, from your child's point of view. As we explained in the earlier section about our core assumptions, experience suggests that most challenging behaviour does have some sort of meaning. You need to pool the information that you have collected about the settings, triggers and results. Equally, you need to take into account what you already know about your child. Ask yourself the following questions.

- Could the behaviour be telling you something about your child's feelings or experience of a particular situation – is the behaviour a way of expressing these feelings?
- Is he using the behaviour as a way of escaping from the situation or avoiding some demand?
- Is the behaviour his way of getting something that he needs or wants – some object or activity, stimulation or excitement, social contact or attention?

In Chapter 6, we look more closely at a range of possible meanings or purposes that may underlie challenging behaviour. As the examples below illustrate, the same behaviour may have widely different purposes. We should also stress that there may be behaviours that simply do not seem to make any sense. Even if you are not able to come up with any firm ideas at Step 5, the thinking and observing that you have done for the earlier steps will still be useful. You may at least have some idea of the factors that influence your child's behaviour. The next steps are about bringing some of these factors under your control.

Case study

Lisa slapped people. She was interested in interacting with others, but had no way of making contact and initiating interaction. Eventually, it proved possible to turn her slap into a stroke.

Neil slapped people. It seemed to happen when he was unsure what to do or when he got stuck with a toy or activity. Teaching him the phrase 'Help me' made a significant difference.

Tom slapped people. The problem regularly cropped up in the playground, usually when he felt that others had cheated at a game (which invariably meant that they were not playing it the way he thought it should be played). A group of classmates have been recruited to play with Tom, starting with fairly formal games. With their help (and the playground supervisors') Tom is being encouraged to opt out when he starts to feel anxious or angry.

Ryan slapped people. It usually meant he got the toy that he wanted. Excluding him from the playroom for two minutes and ensuring that the victim was comforted and given his choice of toys made some difference. Combining this with a rota for the favourite toys and time limits for turns seemed to make a major difference (favourite toys were illustrated on a chart, with children's names stuck against them in sequence).

Planning for change

Just thinking in terms of settings, triggers and results often sparks ideas about how to tackle your child's challenging behaviour. However, as we stressed in the introduction to the Eight-step Plan, it is important to think and plan systematically. Ideally, any plan of action needs to include a strand from each of the final three steps of the Plan.

Step 6: Prevention

This is *the* most important element in any plan of action. Especially with children with autistic spectrum disorders, prevention is usually significantly easier than dealing with a problem once it has actually occurred or become established. Chapters 3, 4 and 5 explore a range of preventive strategies in detail. By looking at the STAR factors and thinking about the questions posed in Step 5, you may already be in a position to answer some of the key questions below.

- Is it possible to actually avoid some of the settings and triggers, if these seem to involve demands and expectations that your child is not equipped to deal with?
- Is there a way to reduce demands and triggers and then gradually raise or reintroduce them a step at a time?
- Can the settings and triggers be altered? Will higher levels of structure help? Do expectations need to be made clearer or more explicit? Will advance warnings and reminders of incentives help?
- What can you learn from the settings where the problem does not occur?

Step 7: New skills and behaviour

The focus of this step is on helping your child learn new skills and encouraging other more acceptable or constructive types of behaviour. It means thinking about what you want your child to do rather than not do.

- What do you want him to be doing at times when he is currently behaving in a difficult way?
- What skills might help him to cope better with problem situations?
- How could he get the same or better pay-offs, but in a more acceptable and constructive way?

This is also the stage at which you need to think about how you and your child will make the small steps that will gradually lead to greater flexibility. Chapters 5 and 6 offer a range of suggestions for tackling these questions.

Step 8: Changing the results

The motivation behind much challenging behaviour is the fact that it achieves particular results or pay-offs for your child. This may not happen each and every time and we may have difficulty understanding why the results are so appealing to him. Nonetheless, if your child behaves in a certain way fairly consistently, we have to either assume that there is something in it for him or that the behaviour is telling us something about his reactions to the situation. The practicalities of changing the results of behaviours are explored in Chapters 8 and 9, but the following questions provide a starting point.

- How do we encourage the behaviour that we want to replace the problem behaviour?
- How can we make sure that the replacement behaviour achieves the same or even better results for the same or less effort?
- What rewards or pay-offs are we able to offer and do these compare to the ones that the behaviour is earning for him at the moment?
- Can we find a way to stop the behaviour resulting in the pay-off so that his motivation to behave in that way is reduced?
- Can we impose any cost so as to discourage the problem behaviour?

Looking after yourself

Constantly dealing with challenging behaviour is extremely demanding. Even when things are going reasonably well, you may feel as if you have to be on your guard all the time, watching out for the warning signs, stepping in to defuse difficult situations or just wondering or worrying about when the next explosion is going to happen. In the heat of the moment, you may find that your child's behaviour provokes in you a whole range of intense and very basic feelings. Sometimes these can be quite overwhelming and even frightening and you may well wonder if you 'ought' to be feeling like this. On the basis of our discussions with parents and teachers, and in our own work with challenging youngsters, this range of feelings can include anxiety, anger, fear, depression, embarrassment, frustration, guilt, isolation, blame, rejection – and many variations on these themes. Even if you only experience feelings like these occasionally or to a relatively mild degree, it can take its toll on your ability to cope.

It is essential to be aware of your own stress levels and important to avoid losing sight of your own needs. For your own sake, as well as for your child's, it is important that you look after yourself. You may find it helpful to keep the following in mind.

- Do not be too hard on yourself. Whatever your plans and intentions, you will not always respond to your child as rationally and reasonably as you hope or feel you ought. You may not always handle situations as smoothly or skilfully as you would like.
- Be realistic about your goals. When change does occur, it will take place slowly, in small steps, and there are bound to be set-backs and plateaux. Try to keep your goals modest and geared to the short term.
- Give yourself (and your child) credit for any movement in the right direction (however small the step might seem).
- Try to stay aware of how you are coping and responding in situations where your child is displaying challenging behaviour. Watch out especially for these warning signs:
  - expecting or aiming to be the perfect parent or teacher
  - expecting to manage every incident successfully
  - feeling that you always have to be in total control of the situation
  - always blaming yourself, or your child, when a difficult situation has arisen
  - treating every set-back as a disaster.
- If you do find that some of these are becoming your habitual style of reacting or thinking, then you may be in danger of trapping yourself in an upward spiral of stress.
- Difficult though it can be, it is important to try to make some time just for yourself. It is not only your right, it is also an essential ingredient in looking after yourself.
- Parents of children with difficulties are particularly at risk of becoming isolated from friends and extended family. Teachers may also find it hard to seek support from colleagues. Finding and maintaining some form of support from others and trying to stay connected to other people can make a crucial difference to your ability to cope.

How to get the most from this book

You will almost certainly want to dip into the chapters that follow, to see if any of the case studies provide ideas for the particular problem that concerns you most. Before doing so, however, we would strongly recommend that you work your way through the Eight-step Plan. There are two important reasons for doing this:

■ you may well find that, by doing so, you begin to generate ideas of your own that fit your particular circumstances better than the examples provided

■ Unless you have some idea of the function that your child's behaviour is serving, it will be difficult to tell if the strategy described in a case study will actually be appropriate and helpful. As we emphasised in our discussion of Step 5, identical behaviours can have very different purposes, so may need to be tackled in very different ways.

Once you have worked your way through the eight steps of the Plan, try to think in terms of the three key ingredients as you draw up your plan of action. These are:

■ **prevention** – covered in Chapters 3, 4 and 5
■ **new skills and behaviour** – covered in Chapters 6 and 7
■ **changing the results** – covered in Chapters 8 and 9.

3
Communicating expectations – getting the message across
Introduction

A vital first step in preventing or dealing with challenging behaviour is to make sure that we have a clear idea about what behaviour we *do* and *do not* want. We then have to find a way of getting this message across to your child in a way that he can really understand.

It can be very hard for a child with an autistic spectrum disorder to understand what is expected in any particular situation. Some problems arise because your child is simply unaware of, or confused about, expectations. We may not even be aware of all the 'rules' in a given situation (until your child fails to fit in with them!) and, in the heat of the moment, we may not make a particularly good job of communicating them. This can be a problem for children with autistic spectrum disorders for a whole variety of reasons.

- In many situations, the 'rules' that govern how children are expected to behave can be very difficult to put into words or tend to be taken for granted so no one thinks to spell them out.
- Even if a child is successful in learning a rule or a 'script' for dealing with a particular situation, he may have difficulties in applying it flexibly to new situations or recognising when it is not appropriate (or not working).
- Whatever else we do when dealing with challenging behaviour, most of us rely heavily on language – to tell, persuade, explain (and threaten!) As we outlined in Chapter 1, almost all children with autistic spectrum disorders have some degree of difficulty in understanding spoken language.
- Most of us find it difficult to stay cool when faced with seriously challenging behaviour. We tend to talk more loudly, more quickly. Our facial expressions and gestures also tend to get 'louder'. All of this may make it more difficult for the child with an autistic spectrum disorder to attend to and take in what we are saying: watching our ever-changing facial expressions may be far more interesting than listening to our words!
- In the heat of the moment, we may be more inclined to focus on what we want the child to *stop* doing rather than on what we want him to do instead. Also, children with autistic spectrum disorders may have genuine difficulty in working out what we *do* want, even if they understand what we do *not* want.

Watching your language

It is important to back up your language with other, non-verbal ways of putting the message across. Some suggestions are included later on. However, because we all tend to rely fairly heavily on spoken language, it is essential for us to monitor the language we use and give the child the best chance of making sense of it.

In order to do this, a vital first step is to get as clear a picture as possible of your child's level of understanding of language. It can be very easy to overestimate this. Many children with autistic spectrum disorders have special skills or seem to learn some things quite readily. Very frequently, these areas of strength involve visual skills and it can be very tempting to jump to conclusions about their understanding of language. These same visual skills also mean that such children can be very good at picking up extra clues to the meaning of what you are saying or learning routines. They may have much greater difficulty with the same type of language if the clues provided by familiar routines and objects are not there. It is also not uncommon for children who develop speech to use language that is actually ahead of their level of comprehension. This makes it very easy to overestimate their level of understanding. For all these reasons, it is important to try and work out what your child can understand – what range of words to use, how many 'bits' of instruction to give at a time and the length and complexity of the sentences he can respond to. Your child's speech and language therapist or teacher should be able to help you clarify these.

To give your child the best chance of understanding your spoken language, try to follow the guidelines below.

- **Match your language to your child's level of understanding** This applies generally as some children with autistic spectrum disorders find it very frustrating and stressful to continually have to cope with language that is pitched at too high a level. Indeed, this alone may trigger challenging behaviour. It is even more important to do this once a problem situation has begun to develop.
- **Get your child's attention before you give any instruction** Teaching your child to respond to his or her name is a very important step, both in managing behaviour and developing understanding of communication.
- **More is less – be brief and put things simply** As a general rule, the less language you use the better. Also, the simpler the language, the more chance there is of your child understanding and responding. This applies particularly if your child is becoming agitated, angry or anxious – these states are all likely to reduce his levels of understanding of language (as they would for us too).
- **Give your child time** Make sure that you allow your child time to process an instruction. Deliberately leave a longer gap than you would when talking to most children. Rushing in with more instructions or efforts to persuade and reason may cause overload.
- **Use repetition** Do not necessarily assume that you have got to find another way of phrasing your request (especially if you have followed the earlier steps in this guidance) – try simply repeating it.
- **Save reasoning for later** Though we would probably all prefer to rely on reasoning and explanation, this may well not be successful in the heat of the moment, even with children who have relatively good understanding of language.
- **Split your instructions into separate parts** You may need to use very simple sentences, leaving out some of the small 'in between' words. For some children it is necessary to build up the sentence by introducing the key word first (such as, 'train set' ... 'put train set away' ... 'put train set away in cupboard').
- **Be concrete and specific** This is especially important when mentioning behaviours that you disapprove of. 'No hitting' is much clearer than 'Don't be naughty.'
- **Use positive instructions** Tell your child what you *do* want. This is much more helpful to your child than a negative request and may actually be easier to understand. Compare 'Eat your food' with 'Don't play with your food.'

■ **Watch your 'turns of phrase'** It is actually very difficult to monitor your use of non-literal language, and almost impossible to avoid using at least some. At the very least, try to avoid putting things indirectly. This can be a cause of difficulties in itself. Pat Howlin gives the example of a child who did exactly as she was told when her teacher said 'Paint the child sitting next to you'! This is also likely to be a problem once a difficult situation has begun to develop. Some of us may be inclined to use phrases such as 'Would you like to ... ?', when what we really mean is 'Please do ...'. It may not be surprising, therefore, that we get 'no' for an answer.

Case study

Alan's mum had a nice chatty style and she felt very uncomfortable about sounding as if she was ordering her son about. She always used his name first, before telling him anything. He was clearly aware that she was trying to get some sort of message across, but was often not sure what that message was. This seemed to cause him frustration and he would often lose his temper and slap her. It turned out that she routinely used quite long sequences, such as 'Alan, love, shall we go to the park? Let's get your wellies on and we'll take some bread for the ducks.' Once Alan's mum got over her inhibitions, she found that 'Alan ... wellies on ... park' worked a lot better.

Being explicit

Many problems occur because your child is unclear about exactly how he is expected to behave in a given situation or what is wanted from him. This applies especially when youngsters have to respond to and cope with other people. In social situations, expectations and norms are usually unspoken. They may actually be so complicated and subtle that it is extremely difficult to even describe them, let alone teach them to someone. Think about explaining to a child how to go about joining in with other children or how much and when you should look at someone when you are speaking to them.

Most children seem to pick up many of these skills intuitively – no one has to spell out expectations to them, let alone teach them directly. Children with autistic spectrum disorders, however, can have substantial difficulty picking up the unwritten expectations and the unspoken signals that other children are often able to sense. They may experience uncertainty and anxiety in ambiguous situations where the ground rules are unclear or appear to shift unpredictably. This anxiety may trigger challenging behaviour. Sometimes they simply get it wrong – they do not behave as others expect them to, or they may disrupt what is going on. This may be viewed as challenging or may create a difficult situation that then escalates.

It is therefore important to look for ways of being really clear and explicit about what is expected, not allowed and the consequences of behaving in a particular way.

Spelling out the rules

Talking in terms of 'rules' may seem rather formal or even authoritarian. Certainly some parents and teachers may well feel quite uncomfortable thinking in these terms. However, children with autistic spectrum disorders seem to find it easier to cope when we spell out our expectations concerning behaviour in a specific, concise and unambiguous way. Framing these as relatively impersonal 'dos and don'ts' also seems to add authority.

We also use the word 'rules' to refer to the norms and expectations that guide much of our behaviour in social situations. When we try to make these unwritten rules explicit, we face three difficult tasks.

- Getting some idea of what the expectations and ways of doing things in a given situation actually are and then where things are likely to break down for the child we have in mind.
- Because there are no hard and fast rules and there is always some flexibility, the second task is to come up with what are often rough and ready guidelines. These may seem rather clumsy and artificial. However, if they give your child a way of achieving his goal in that situation, without making him more conspicuous than before, they can be a very helpful way to reduce anxiety and prevent challenging behaviour.
- Finally, we have to find a way of teaching a child the rules and the skills needed.

Think about these guidelines when considering how to go about spelling out the rules for your child. Bear in mind the following points.

- With young children, you may need to start with very simple, clear and consistent rules. A rule such as, 'You can only touch members of your family' may seem quite artificial and inflexible. However, you need to anticipate what may become a problem in the future: a youngster who kisses and cuddles strangers at four may still be seen as 'cute', but this behaviour will draw quite a different reaction when he is ten.
- Try to personalise the rule to your child's situation and particular needs.
- It is generally easier to start with more restrictive rules and then gradually relax them than it is to start off relaxed and then become more restrictive.
- The older the child, the more chance he has of being able to cope with exceptions or learning about situations where a modified version of the rule applies. Pat Howlin describes a youngster who, as a result of an accident, needed to be taken directly to hospital from school. Problems arose because he would not allow doctors to examine him. Earlier in his life he had had a tendency to strip off at school, so his parents had successfully dealt with this by using a 'clothes can't be removed without our permission' rule.
- As we mentioned above, with children who have sufficient understanding, it can certainly be helpful to talk in terms of 'rules' or generalisations about what 'everyone' does. As well as adding authority, this can help to play down the personal element in the situation – that is, you are not asking your child to behave in a certain way because of your personal whim, but because that is how children are expected to behave in that situation.
- Try to find a way to represent rules visually. With children who can read, a brief, written 'code of conduct' may be helpful. This can be carried or displayed in an appropriate place. Symbols and cartoons can also be used.

Steven was in a busy class of six-year-olds. When he was stuck or had finished his work, he would go and hover near his teacher. He did not know how to get her attention, often would not be in her line of sight and was just as likely to stand staring at the wall as look at her. There was usually a crowd of children waiting for her and it was very easy to overlook Steven. To deal with the problem, he was given a set of 'rules' – how close to stand, where, what to do to draw the teacher's attention to him and how to tell when she had noticed (but needed him to wait his turn). This was rehearsed and presented in cartoon form. Though it looked rather wooden, it did achieve its purpose and it was later possible to modify steps (for instance, so that he no longer tapped his teacher's arm, but waited for a gap and then said her name).

Keeping consequences in mind

It is just as important to be clear and explicit about the consequences of behaving in a certain way – particularly finding ways to remind your child of any incentives or positive consequences that you are using. When faced with something that they would prefer to avoid or that makes them anxious, children with autistic spectrum disorders often seem to have difficulty seeing past the situation. They may not anticipate the treat that usually follows or the more pleasurable activity that comes later, but instead focus on what is happening now.

For this reason, it is always helpful to remind your child of any treat or preferred activity that will follow whatever you are asking of him. For many parents, an enormous breakthrough comes when their child is able to understand the phrase 'First ..., then ...'. This seems to help in two ways. First, it assists him in understanding that the present activity does actually have an end point, rather than going on forever – the idea of endings is something that some children with autistic spectrum disorders seem to have difficulty in grasping. Second, a reminder about the following, favoured activity may also help motivate him to complete the first task. This strategy is also a way of dealing with any anxiety that there may be about 'what's coming next'.

Verbal reminders about consequences are only one way of getting this particular message across (see below for ways to use your child's visual strengths).

Shaun was eight, severely autistic and had additional learning difficulties. He was intent on following his own agenda. If any demand was made (especially if it interrupted his obsessions) or any wish was frustrated (if another child had a toy he wanted, for example) he would resort to kicking, hitting and scratching. Although he seemed to be able to understand sentences with three main elements, the situation improved when verbal instructions were simplified to a 'first ..., then ...' format. Using a simple visual system to get across the same message seemed even more effective. He began to learn that he first had to do what the adult asked and then he could have a turn at his preferred activity. Additionally, his teachers and parents used a chair (covered with a yellow cloth) for occasions when he hurt someone. He was prompted to remain on the chair until calm, following which the 'first ..., then...' cards were used. The yellow cloth that had been used to cover the chair was then introduced in other settings and was eventually hung on the wall. Drawing his attention to it if he was becoming angry often seemed to have a calming effect.

Case study

By the time she was 13, Jenny had learned the art of the sit-down protest during shopping trips with her parents. She was also clearly aware that she was now far too big to be moved bodily. Her parents were not sure that she understood, or could remember, their promise of a favourite video as soon as they got home. They decided to shorten the shopping expeditions and allow Jenny to take the video case with her, as a reminder of the 'treat' that would be hers as soon as they got home. This seemed to help and they were then able to gradually build up the time they spent in town.

Writing 'Social Stories'

It is actually very difficult to come up with general rules about social behaviour that apply across settings. The help that any child needs will depend on the particular difficulties that he experiences in a given situation. What are usually needed are individualised 'scripts' – guidance on what to do and how to behave in that specific situation.

Carol Gray has developed an approach that involves working with the child to produce a short, illustrated story. The story aims to help develop the child's understanding of a given situation *and* provide specific strategies for coping with it.

The approach is based on careful observation of the problem situation – paying particular attention to the point at which things seem to break down. The adult needs to think about what the child would need to be able to understand and do in order to cope better. These observations are combined with knowledge of your child to produce an individualised script for coping with the situation. This is phrased in terms of generalisations about what people usually do in such situations (and why) and explicit guidance on what your child is expected to do. The stories also often include content that is intended to develop your child's understanding of other people's perspectives. (Detailed guidance for Carol Gray's method can be found in the reference included in the Further Reading section.)

Provided your child can understand the language and illustrations that are used in the story, he does not need to be able to read – an adult can regularly read and rehearse the story with him. Stories can also be recorded so your child can 'read' through the book and listen to the tape.

Social Stories are also very useful in helping to prepare children for change. They can help to familiarise children with the situation that they are going to encounter. They can also be used to give guidelines on how to behave in the new situation and so help to create an expectation of confidence and success.

Ruth used to have difficulties settling back to sleep if she woke in the night. Her parents gradually slipped into the habit of letting her get into their bed and so, seven years later, Ruth was still sleeping with her parents. The problem seemed to have much more to do with her rigidity than any fear of being on her own. Unlike her parents, Ruth now settled easily at night, slept well and was raring to go by 5am. Though her understanding of speech was quite limited, she was a relatively good reader. It was decided to make use of her reading *and* her rigidity. This social story was prepared, illustrated, and read with her by her parents and teacher.

When girls are nine years old they are very grown up. They learn new things. They do new things.
Nine-year-old girls have their own bedrooms. They sleep in their own beds. They sleep in their own bedrooms.
I am nine soon.
I have got my own bedroom.
When I am nine, I will get ready for bed at 8 o'clock. I will get ready for bed in my bedroom.
At 8.30, Mummy and Daddy will tuck me up, give me a kiss and say, 'Night, night.' They will leave the door open and leave the lamp on.
I will stay in my own bedroom. I will sleep in my own bedroom.
At 6 o'clock I can get up and go downstairs.
I will feel very grown up.

Ruth moved into her own bedroom on her ninth birthday – and has slept there ever since.

Backing up your spoken language

Understanding of language only develops very slowly in many children with autistic spectrum disorders. Even where this seems to be relatively good, it may take the child more time and more deliberate effort to tune in to someone else's speech and make sense of it. Whereas spoken words last for no more than a few thousandths of a second, a picture or symbol is permanent and your child has more time to take in its meaning. This means that the message is less likely to be missed because of a shift in attention or anxiety getting in the way. Because your child can choose to look again and process the message in his own time and in his own way, his independence is increased. It can therefore be very helpful to make use of the visual skills that are often relatively strong in children with autistic spectrum disorders. Indeed, for many, this seems to be their preferred mode. Finding ways in which to present requests or reminders about rules and expectations in a visual form can greatly increase the likelihood of a successful outcome. Here are some ideas.

■ Pictures (or even objects chosen to stand for certain activities) can be a very good way to establish an understanding of 'First ..., then ...' statements (this is described in more detail in the next chapter).

■ Once an understanding of pictures has been built up, they can sometimes be used to remind children of specific rewards that you may want to provide for coping with specific situations. This can be very useful for things such as shopping trips or car journeys where it may be difficult to actually provide worthwhile incentives for some children. Having a picture of a favourite activity or the cover of the video that he can watch once he gets home can help give motivation and bridge the gap.

- A small range of simple signs (especially if used consistently in home and at school) may also help your child to understand and respond to spoken requests. The meaning of signs and gestures (as well as pictures and symbols) may actually be accessed more directly and immediately by the brain. As a result, they may convey a greater sense of urgency and command. This said, it is important to note that signs do share one of the disadvantages of speech – they last for only a very short time.
- Simple symbols (in the style of road signs) can be used to highlight key rules or commands. If you happen to be working on a particular behaviour, one or two of these symbols can be on permanent display or introduced at critical points in a situation. Older children with reading skills may be able to cope with these in a simple written format. This overcomes a problem shared by signs and speech – their very brief duration. If your child is not paying full attention, the message may have come and gone before he has had time to take it in.

Case study

Umar had a passion for *Thomas the Tank Engine* – and for waking up his parents unreasonably early. Getting him to bed was no easier than keeping him there in the mornings. Fortunately, at seven years old he could tell the time. His parents made two 'Thomas' clocks for him. The 'morning' clock had its hands set at 7am and included a rising sun among the train illustrations. The 'bedtime' clock incorporated a moon. His parents knew that they could not *make* him sleep, but they did make sure that his bedroom contained plenty of toys that he could entertain himself with. Umar was shown how to tell when the times on his clocks tallied with the times on the real clock in his bedroom. He was taught to stay in his room until the 'morning' clock tallied with the real one, and to start getting ready for bed when his 'bedtime' clock and the real one said the same time. This seemed to work much better than simply telling him what time he was allowed up and reminding him to look at the time.

Case study

Leanne seemed to understand written language better than spoken language. She was very keen on books (to the point of almost being obsessed with having one in her hand). Frequently, she took them out into the garden with her. They sometimes seemed to get in the way of her play and often ended up wet, torn or dirty. Her mum did not want to have to nag her or keep a constant eye on her comings and goings to the garden. She also wanted to avoid the tantrums that occasionally resulted when a book was taken from Leanne. A written reminder at eye level on the kitchen door, plus a symbol showing a black outline of a book with a red line through it, seemed to do the trick.

Staying in control

Communicating expectations or giving instructions is not just about *what* you say but is also about the *way* that you say it. Not only the particular choice of words, but the tone of voice and the message that your facial expression and body language put across. When faced with a child who is already anxious or angry, it is important for adults to at least appear to be in control of themselves and the situation. This can be exceptionally difficult and no-one succeeds all the time. However, if you can manage it, an impression of calmness and control can reassure your child that the situation is still safe and that you still have the power to restore some degree of order. Even when the situation has not become critical, an instruction delivered in a calm, confident way is more likely to be responded to than one uttered in anger. This is discussed in more detail in Chapter 5, but the tips given below may be helpful.

- **Try to give instructions 'with the emotions turned off'** This was the advice of Hans Asperger, the Austrian psychiatrist after whom the syndrome was named. Using a relatively calm, neutral tone of voice seems to help a child to focus on the meaning of what the adult is saying. With older children, who have relatively good understanding of language, this reduces the risk of them reacting to the perceived mood of the adult, which is often a way for them to avoid the issue that you are trying to deal with.

- **Use your body language to calm, not confront** This applies particularly once you feel your child has passed the point of no return, when your main priority is to stop the situation getting any worse. Your tone of voice (if you have managed to keep it relatively calm) needs to be mirrored by your other body language. This means trying to avoid frequent changes, or extremes, of facial expression. It is also helpful to avoid intense or prolonged eye contact. Do not crowd or loom over your child. Though this may well take a great deal of self-control, try to keep your shoulders, arms and hands down and stay relatively still.

- **Try to manage your thinking** One of the most important (and most difficult) strategies for staying calm is to keep track of your own state of mind. Watch out especially for the ways of thinking that we mentioned at the end of Chapter 2, under the heading 'Looking after yourself'. If the problem is one that you have encountered before and you have managed to make sense of why your child is behaving in this way, you may need to remind yourself. In the heat of the moment, it can be very tempting to think that your child is deliberately behaving in this way just to torment you.

- **Slow down** It is almost always useful to try and slow yourself (and the situation) down. Pause after you have given an instruction – that space will help you think and makes it more likely that you will feel (or look) like you are in control. Just as importantly, it will give your child space and time to make sense of the instruction.

- **Defusing the situation may be more important than getting your own way** You may be able to defuse the situation by providing a distraction – simply sidestepping and trying to shift your child's attention to something else. (Many of the strategies suggested in Chapter 5 focus on ways of defusing and distracting.)

4
Using structure

Introduction

Children with autist... ...lmost every book or piece of advice concerning them w... ...d there is a great deal of evidence that structure doe... ...t helps in preventing challenging behaviour. The amount an... ...vary from child to child. It is also important to work to... ...structure – increasing flexibility is an importa... ...core problems in autistic spectrum disorders. To... ...s useful to raise the level of structure in your child'... ...feel rather restrictive and rigid, especially in the home...

If you think about th... ...n Chapter 1, it becomes clear why structure is helpful.

- Language prob... ...nake sense of what is expected from him. Prov... ...y of getting the message across without relying... ...ibutes to your child's independence.
- The difficulty... ...igs, intentions and motives makes it very hard to p... ...– or to understand why they did what they did... ...the form of routines or 'scripts') can help redu... ...results from having to deal with others.
- Understanding... ...ppen, as well as the order in which it is going to happ... ...for children with autistic spectrum disorders. Pro... ...quence seem to combine with problems of imagination.'... ...ven later this morning or this afternoon – can seem very u... ...ries.
- Providing structure also h... ...e the child's need for 'sameness'. Structure (and therefore predictability) can help... ...ce your child's levels of anxiety. This may well reduce his need to impose his own routines and rituals or retreat into obsessions.

Finding the right level of structure for your child may involve some trial and error, and such high levels of organisation and routine may not, at first, suit your particular style. Without quite high levels of structure, however, children with autistic spectrum disorders seem to experience raised levels of anxiety and frustration. This means that challenging behaviour may be triggered more easily and routines and repetitive behaviours may be harder to interrupt. What we mean by 'structure' and some of the methods we advocate for putting it in place are described in the sections that follow.

Case study

As dinnertime got closer, Aseasha would become increasingly preoccupied with whether or not her class would be first into the dining room. If she heard other classes passing the door of her classroom en route to the dining room or if she got there and other children were already seated, she would throw herself on the floor and scream in rage. Her preoccupation with being first seemed, in part, to be a response to her uncertainty and anxiety about the pattern of events at dinnertime. Two things seemed to help. First, she was allowed to always sit in the same place in the dining hall (a special placemat was used and her name was taped to the chair). Second, a chart was devised that showed her the order in which classes were going for their dinner. To begin with, her class was allowed to go first, but, gradually, the order was altered and Aseasha became much better at tolerating this – as long as she knew what was going to happen.

Avoiding triggers

This is such an obvious and commonsense aspect of structuring the environment that it is easily overlooked. This, though, is why it is important to have thought about your child's behaviour in terms of the STAR framework. If you can reliably identify triggers for challenging behaviour and if it is possible to avoid them (at least in the short to medium term), then you may have gone a good way towards resolving at least some of the difficulties. Now, these are obviously very big 'ifs', but it is worth giving a bit of thought to some of the points that follow.

The physical environment

This is a useful starting point. Your child may not have the communication skills to let you know if he is physically uncomfortable or distressed as a result of some aspect of the environment. Even when children do have language, they may not always realise that an adult cannot know that there is a problem unless told about it.

In Chapter 1, we mentioned the problem of oversensitivity to sounds, and it is sometimes possible to organise your child's physical environment so that these are avoided. Of course, it may not be possible to eliminate some sounds but, for example, playing a tape of soothing sounds or music may mask some night-time noises that unsettle children. It is sometimes possible to use a social story to explain the origin of a particular sound or prepare your child for occasional, intrusive sounds such as fire alarms.

Overcrowding or visual clutter in the environment may have similar effects. In the next section we discuss ways in which it is possible to gradually improve your child's tolerance but, initially, the emphasis may need to be on you spotting these aspects of the environment and trying to reduce your child's exposure to them.

Mark's mum wanted him to attend the local playgroup. Unfortunately, this was held in a large church hall. The group was very popular and sessions were fairly busy. Mark seemed to be completely overwhelmed by the large space and the noise from the uncarpeted floorboards. Fortunately, there was a smaller side room, usually used for storytime, which could be reached by a separate door. Mark gradually built up his time at playgroup in this separate room, with other children and slightly noisier activities being slowly introduced. The door through to the hall was left open and one or two tempting activities were placed in sight. Gradually Mark would make occasional, short excursions to the edge of the hall. He never became relaxed about this, but instead of standing with his fingers in his ears and screaming, he learned to retreat to the side room if things got too much.

Reducing demands

When a particular situation seems to regularly trigger challenging behaviour, it is useful to take stock of the demands that the situation is making on your child. Think about what he is expected to do in that situation and ask yourself if this is reasonable, given his age and skills. The demands may be in terms of actions – things your child is expected to actually do. Equally, they could be in terms of what your child is expected to not do – things that we tend not to see as skills at all, such as waiting, doing nothing or refraining from some behaviour.

Sometimes the situations and the demands are unavoidable (some of the approaches described in other sections of this book may be helpful with these). However, it is always useful to ask yourself 'Is this a battle worth fighting at the moment?' You are bound to want to make life as normal as possible for yourself, your child and for your family, but there may be some situations that you can and should avoid, at least for the time being.

Other people are not just an important element of the physical environment. Even if they make no demands at all, their very presence may represent a particular source of stress. Your child may still be anxious about what they might do or say or might simply see them as bafflingly unpredictable. Later sections of this book suggest strategies that may help your child learn the skills needed to cope better, but in the short term it may be necessary to look for ways to reduce your child's exposure to these situations.

Problems often occur where the demand on your child is to 'do nothing'. This can be difficult for all children, but, when they are 'doing nothing', they are often actually entertaining themselves. They may be daydreaming, catching other people's eyes or watching 'that funny lady'. Children with autistic spectrum disorders may not be able to pass time in this way and may not understand that the situation is just temporary. Providing them with some form of distraction to help fill these gaps may be all that is needed to overcome any problems that occur at such times. It may be appropriate to use some forms of obsessional interest for this purpose.

Case study

David attended mainstream secondary school and got very anxious and agitated when moving between classrooms. It often took him a long time to settle down at the start of a lesson and then his stress level would rise as the end of the lesson approached. Other students were generally very supportive towards David, and the problem was more to do with the hustle and bustle and what others might do rather than because something had actually happened. Things improved considerably when it was arranged that David would leave lessons slightly early and arrive slightly late (taking refuge in the library in between). Any problems resulting from the missed time in lessons were more than compensated for by his calmer state and improved ability to concentrate in lessons.

Reducing temptations

Sometimes it is not that the setting triggers challenging behaviour as such, it is the fact that a particular environment contains temptations or opportunities that then lead to difficulties. This undoubtedly applies to all children and is why most parents childproof their homes to some degree. However, it may need to be done more systematically and comprehensively for children with autistic spectrum disorders.

Problems are particularly likely to occur in relation to strong obsessions. Challenging behaviour may be triggered by your child, for instance, catching sight of something that is particularly good for spinning or spotting an especially tempting ball of fluff. The actual obsessive behaviour is not so much the problem, but the strength of the determination to have immediate access to the item is. For this reason, when going into unfamiliar environments, it may be helpful to take along a stock of your child's favourite objects or activities. If something then triggers your child's particular preoccupation, you are in a position to supply what is needed rather than having to deal with the problems that may result from your child helping himself. A variation on this approach (discussed in more detail in Chapter 6) is to make sure that your child has access to his obsession, but on your terms rather than his.

Case study

At six years old, Martin had very few skills for entertaining himself. His greatest pleasure seemed to be the sound and sensation he got from ripping paper and letting the pieces flutter to the ground. Any books or magazines that were left in his reach got this treatment, and his family (especially his older brother) were getting fed up with having to be on their guard all the time. They finally dealt with the difficulty by creating a den behind the settee for Martin and stocking it with mail order catalogues that he was allowed to tear. Whenever he was found tearing something that he should not, he was firmly stopped, taken to his den and shown that he was allowed to tear the paper that was there. His parents would also take one of these catalogues with them when they visited other houses with Martin and this seemed to reduce the risk of him damaging other people's things.

Structuring the environment

Removing temptations and triggers is one way of structuring the environment in order to prevent challenging behaviour from occurring. Other aspects of the organisation of the environment can also have a crucial influence on the behaviour of children with autistic spectrum disorders. Some children seem to panic if there is too much space. At the other extreme, an environment that is too cluttered and full of distraction makes it hard for your child to grasp what is expected or remain on track. Thinking about these difficulties can make a great deal of difference to how well your child copes, particularly with the school environment.

By structuring the environment, you aim to do three things:

- reduce possible sources of distraction and confusion that may get in the way of your child's understanding of what is required
- remove, where possible, potential triggers or temptations that could lead your child into situations where challenging behaviour might occur
- provide permanent visual cues or reminders that help your child to understand what is expected – what he is supposed to be doing, where he is supposed to be and how he should organise himself (just think about the expectations that are communicated by the physical layout and contents of the various rooms in the home or school – the toilet, soft play area, kitchen and so on).

By providing structure, you are dealing directly with some of your child's core difficulties. You reduce the demands on his understanding and use of language and memory and make the most of any visual strengths that he may have.

A place for everything and everything in its place

With young children, it can be helpful to build up a link between a particular activity and the place where it happens. This gives your child another way of knowing what is happening. It can also build up a form of habit as your child learns to behave in a certain way, in a certain place, hopefully with less need for you to repeat instructions or supervise. As with building up routines, this is a way of making the most of your child's tendency to prefer fixed patterns. Ideally, this means trying to have physically separate places for independent work, group activities, play, self-care and so on. Here are some ideas you might like to try.

- Even in homes (or classrooms) that do not have the luxury of separate areas for separate activities, it is still possible to provide visual cues about what should be happening. For example a different coloured tablecloth or mat on the same table can be used to make it clear that messy play has ended and that it is now time to eat.
- A variation on this theme is to make sure that the materials used in a given activity are stored in a distinctive container, which is only brought out when that activity is taking place. Even a simple strategy, such as covering the computer with a cloth when it is not available, can be an effective way to get the message across.
- Some children have problems with large or cluttered spaces – knowing where to sit on the carpet at storytime or where to stand in the hall are common examples. It is often helpful to provide a carpet tile or a hoop, so the child knows where to be. This may reduce any anxiety connected with not knowing, or not being able to decide where to go. During the activity, it also provides a prompt, which may reduce the likelihood of the child shuffling about, distracting others and ending up in trouble.

- Tape can be used to mark important thresholds that the child should not cross without an adult present. Of course, your child will not understand its significance without a good deal of help from you. He will need to be prompted to stop by the line – and it is essential to reward his doing so generously. The line may eventually act as a reminder and the child may learn to respond to it because of its association with a reward.
- At a very simple level, labelling cupboards and storage spaces with pictures, words or symbols can prevent behaviour problems and help towards greater independence. As well as helping the child to know where things go, they remind the child about the range of options available and where to find particular toys.

Case study

Whenever Nadia saw an open door, she would dash through it. Although she was ten, she was completely unaware of any danger and it was fairly obvious she was doing it because she liked the 'chase'. At school, staff marked the floor just inside the door with a very clear red line and also hung a curtain across the door. This tended to slow Nadia down as she approached the door, so that staff could then prompt her to stop in front of the line. They drew her attention to the line and gave her lots of praise, cuddles and tickles for stopping. If she did manage to get through the door, staff retrieved her, giving her as little attention as possible. Eventually Nadia learned to stop at the line, without the curtain, and seemed to do this when she wanted some sort of special attention from adults. It was important for classroom staff to respond accordingly, but this was much better than having to dash after her.

Creating a workspace

This is one very concrete and helpful instance of the general strategy of linking specific activities to specific locations. In classrooms that are set up especially for the needs of children with autistic spectrum disorders, this may take the form of individual, screened workstations where all independent work is carried out. Even without this level of resources, there are a number of commonsense and inexpensive things that can be done in many classrooms.

This approach may also be helpful at home. You may not particularly want your child to do school-type tasks at home. However, it is likely that at some time you will want to help your child to occupy himself with some sort of appropriate leisure activity for longer periods of time. This can be especially useful with a child who is physically restless. Having a 'play space' may help your child to settle to the activity long enough to begin to get some enjoyment from it. To create a work space:

- try to position your child so that he is away from busy areas, doors, windows and other potential sources of distraction – facing a blank wall is ideal
- see if you can create a physical boundary around the space – it is sometimes possible to reposition furniture to create an 'alcove' – but, if not, think about using screens that can sit on the tabletop (they do not need not be elaborate – cardboard packaging from large appliances is perfectly adequate)
- even if this cannot be done, you may still be able to mark out the boundaries of a workspace in some other way – using a tablecloth, placemat or tape, for example.

Structuring activities

As well as considering the overall layout and organisation of the environment, it is useful to think on a more detailed scale. It is helpful to physically organise tasks so you create a framework that guides your child through the task. This develops independence by reducing the need for adult prompting and supervision. It also reduces the frustration and anxiety of getting in a muddle, of not knowing where you are going or where the end point is. The following are some suggestions for structuring activities.

- Where tasks involve a sequence of activities (especially where they need to happen in a certain order, such as cooking), a sequence of photographic cues can be helpful.
- A task such as clearing the table and organising the washing up may be easier if the child has separate, labelled baskets for clearing the cutlery, then the glasses and then the plates.
- If you are just wanting to encourage your child to play with a wider range of toys for longer periods, then you may want to put, for example, three toys in three separate baskets arranged left to right. You can then teach your child to work along the row of baskets, playing with each toy in turn, then putting discarded toys in a 'finished' basket.
- Any teacher who has been introduced to the TEACCH approach will be familiar with these ideas (for more information, see the book by Eric Schopler and his colleagues listed in the Further Reading section). Work systems that clearly show the child what has to be done and in what order can be exceptionally helpful. With younger children, these can take the form of 'work baskets', as outlined in the last point. With older or more able youngsters, clear written instructions or a sequence of 'job cards' may be all that is needed. Depending on the complexity of the tasks, additional help may be needed, so that the child understands exactly how to go about it and in what order to do the tasks.

Case study

Peter was ten years old and had the physical skills needed to dress himself. He seemed to have become completely dependent on his dad to hand him his clothes and talk (or nag) him through each step. If he was left on his own, he would take forever and often end up with clothes the wrong way round. Things improved a good deal when his dad cut up strips of wallpaper to make 'templates' on which Peter's clothes were laid in the order that he needed to put them on. The templates seemed to act as reminders of 'what next' and allowed his father to leave Peter to do the job on his own. An incentive for getting the job done in a set time limit also seemed to help.

Structuring time – routines and timetables

When we think of structure, we tend to think immediately in terms of what we can see – the physical aspects of the environment. For children with autistic spectrum disorders, it is just as important to think about the way that *time* is organised. They seem to have a particularly strong need to know what is going to happen next, and particular problems with sequences and the organisation of time. This is often the focus of a great deal of repetitive questioning and some children seem to have a remarkable ability to remember when things happened without necessarily having a sense of time. We therefore need to think about the order in which things are done and the ways that they are done – how each step is carried out and the sequence of the steps within an activity. Helping your child understand what is happening and anticipate what is *going* to happen is one of the most important ways in which you can prevent challenging behaviour. It also has the very important spin-off of helping to develop independence.

Setting up routines

The first step in responding to this need is to try and ensure that there is some degree of routine in the way things are done and their order. The levels of detail and consistency that are needed will very much depend on your child and it can be hard to predict what is required. Some children do not seem to mind what happens during the rest of the day, provided that the getting up or going to bed routines are followed exactly. Trying to take the initiative and establish a routine that *you* can live with may be better than allowing your child to impose an arbitrary routine. When there is no particular order, some children seem to pick up on the way that things were done on a particular day and then insist on this being repeated. When this has not been thought through in advance, it may end up being difficult to live with or inappropriate in some way. Ruth's old bedtime routine, described in the case study in the last chapter is a good case in point.

The following are some helpful pointers for setting up routines.

- It is very useful to try to build up self-care routines from the earliest possible stage. Children with autistic spectrum disorders are especially prone to becoming dependent on prompts, so it is important to think these through carefully and try to fade them out systematically. With self-care tasks that involve several steps, a sequence of picture or symbol prompts can be especially useful.
- When you need to prompt any sequence of behaviour, always use the fewest and least intrusive prompts possible: visual prompts (such as a gesture from you) tend to be preferable to verbal prompts; verbal prompts tend to be preferable to physical prompts.
- When you want to fade out the prompts, it can be helpful to fade out the last prompt first. So, if you have had to help your child put his trousers on, prompting his hand movements with your own hands all the way, try getting him to pull them up the last little bit unprompted.
- As well as the benefit of routines creating predictability, they may also help your child to make overall sense of the activity, to see where things are leading and what the point of it all is. As your child becomes familiar with each step, you may find that he shows signs of anticipating, or even initiating, the next step.
- Routines are also a way of helping your child cope with transitions from one activity to another.
- In school, children with autistic spectrum disorders seem to cope better when classroom activities follow a predictable pattern. Specific routines may need to be created for situations that are a regular feature of classroom life. These may include asking for help (as in the case of Steven, described in Chapter 3), clearing away at the end of a session or lesson, what to do when you have finished work, finding a place to sit when entering a classroom or regrouping in the class and so on.
- Even if the class follows a fairly detailed class timetable, a child with an autistic spectrum disorder may need his own personalised routine to help him through each separate activity.
- Social stories are a very good way of explaining the steps in a routine.

Whatever routines you establish, and whether or not your child can understand a visual timetable showing the routine, there is bound to come a time when you want to change it or when circumstances force you to. Ways of introducing change are discussed in some detail in the next chapter, but it is worth emphasising here that, from the early stages, it can be helpful if you have prepared your child for changes by occasionally trying to 'sneak in' a change of order, leaving out a small step or adding a slight variation. At the very least, this will give you a clue about the size of the challenge that may be facing you and your child.

Case study

Like many households, Bobby's was fairly chaotic first thing in the morning. He often ended up, still in his pyjamas, glued to his favourite video with the school minibus waiting outside the house. His parents finally decided to adopt a routine and a few simple rules. Bobby was not allowed downstairs until he was dressed, breakfast always came next and then – and only then – was he allowed to watch the video until the minibus arrived.

Building picture timetables

In the last chapter, we briefly mentioned the use of pictures as a way of helping your child to understand 'First ..., then ...' statements. As well as being a way in which you can negotiate with your child and help him keep a particular incentive in mind, picture timetables are a vital way of structuring time. 'Visual schedules' (as they are often termed) are one of the core techniques of the TEACCH approach and are in widespread use in classrooms in the UK. They use a typical area of strength – visual skills – to tackle a typical area of difficulty – anticipating future events. The following pointers will help you to set up a picture timetable.

- **Pictures or symbols**? First, decide whether or not you are going to actually use pictures. Symbols, line drawings or printed words can also be used and can offer more flexibility. However, do not automatically go for the most advanced system that you think your child can cope with. Even if your child can read, you want something that he can take in at a glance, so pictures or symbols may be easier to access than words.
- **Using objects** With youngsters who do not seem to respond to pictures, it may be possible to use objects that have a direct connection with the activity. An empty crisp packet laminated to a card might represent snack time, dinnertime could be shown by an apron, a deflated armband might signify swimming and so on. It is important to stress that the object of reference, as it is usually referred to, should not be the actual object that is the focus of the activity – it needs to be something that has a close connection with the activity, but is then used to stand for it.
- **Making the connection** Build the link between the activity and the picture (or symbol), starting with only one or two pictures. To establish the connection, you need to show your child the picture every time the activity is about to happen and draw attention to it during the activity as well, using simple, consistent language to label what you are doing. You will know your child understands the picture when he shows signs of anticipation – going to get his coat when shown the photo of the park, for example.
- **Marking endings** It is also helpful to develop a routine to clearly signal the end of an activity. When it has finished, prompt your child to put away any materials that were connected to the activity, then put the photo away in a special box or envelope. Make sure that you also stress the word 'finished'. Understanding that something has ended seems to be especially difficult for some youngsters to grasp.

- **'First ..., then ...'** Once your child understands a range of individual photographs or symbols, you can begin to build up an understanding of the concept and the phrase 'first ..., then ...'. This is an especially helpful step when the second activity is one that your child enjoys, and it is following something that he is not very keen on. It may help to have a set location for this timetable. Stick the two pictures in a top-down or left-right sequence and help your child to take the first of these, while ensuring that he also looks at the second, as you explain the sequence (self-adhesive Velcro is very useful for setting up this type of timetable).

- **'And then ...'** Gradually, it may be possible to build up a 'timetable' that spans half a day or even a whole day. As far as possible, you should encourage your child to check 'what next' for himself, so that he begins to move towards independence. This is a very useful strategy if your child is inclined to ask repeatedly about future events, provided that this is what is really worrying him.

- **Including rewards** If your child is able to grasp even short timetable sequences, it is very useful to include pictures that represent rewards and favourite activities (including times when your child gets the chance to engage in his special interests). In this way, your child receives the reassurance of seeing that he will still get to do his favourite things and can tell when these will be available.

- **Building a routine for using timetables** Your child will need to be shown how to use his timetable, with routines at the start and end of activities. You may want to start with the timetable in a fixed location, with your child going to that place to get the picture for the next activity and returning the 'finished' picture. Older children may need to have portable timetable systems, using ring binders, pictures or symbols on a key ring or the sort of wallet designed for holding credit cards.

Case study

At nine years old, Philip still did not seem to be aware when he needed to use the toilet and showed few signs of recognising what was happening when he was actually 'performing'. There did seem to be some pattern to when he wet or soiled his nappy, so his parents included regular visits to the toilet in his routine and in the picture timetable that they had introduced (timing these to coincide with when he was most likely to go). In addition, they also had a very detailed picture timetable in the toilet, with simple stick-man illustrations for each step of using the toilet. They managed to keep Philip on the toilet for five or ten minutes by letting him play with a favourite toy, and this seemed to help him overcome the anxiety that he seemed to experience to begin with. Though his parents hope that eventually he will become sufficiently aware to know when he needs to use the toilet, this arrangement has improved the situation, making things easier for them and more dignified for Philip.

Case study

Almost every time she went to the supermarket, Vicky would end up attacking her mum, usually grabbing her hair and sometimes managing to pull her mother to the ground. Because she was now too big to physically restrain, Vicky's mother had taken to using sweets as a way of diverting Vicky from these tantrums. However, it now seemed as if Vicky was unable to wait and was using the tantrums as a way of making sure that she got her sweets. The situation improved when her mum began to use two photographs. One showed the shopping trolley, full up and ready to go through the checkout. The second showed Vicky in the car, ready to go home, eating her sweets. Combined with the spoken message 'first shopping, then sweets', this seemed to help Vicky understand the order of events and reassured her that she would get her sweets – but now on her mum's terms.

Jitesh's mother had major problems whenever she needed to take him shopping. He seemed to get very agitated and would then insist on only going to a few shops, in a certain order. At five years old, he was getting too big to be restrained in the buggy. Things got a lot better when Jitesh's mum took photos of each of the shops they regularly visited and used them to prepare him for the shopping expedition. Looking at the photos, talking about the shops and arranging them in sequence seemed to help Jitesh understand and anticipate what was about to happen. Though he still insisted on sticking to a set order, he was a good deal happier and it was possible to get him into a wider range of shops.

Timetables and routines – for fun!

Of course, it is easy to think in terms of a timetable or routine as a list of activities that your child has *got* to do. Indeed, much of this book is about ways in which you can ensure that your child will do the things that you want him to do or he needs to do. However, timetables and routines can also be used to help your child organise his own activities and get the most out of situations where he has a choice of what to do.

Children with autistic spectrum disorders often have problems coping with free choices and free time. They may have trouble thinking of the options, making a choice or may not know how to organise the time so that they can do a variety of things. Giving your child pictures of the various options may help him to make choices.

Once your child has selected a number, these can then be arranged along a timeline in a preferred order, taking account of the time available and the likely duration of the activities. Some children with autistic spectrum disorders seem to prefer even greater levels of structure, with a timer that tells them how long to take for each of the options.

Lee did not seem to know what to do with himself in the evening once the 'coming home from school' and teatime routines were over. He was continually interfering with whatever his older brothers were doing, but never really seemed to want to get properly involved. When they objected to this, there was usually a major tantrum. As soon as his dad got home from work, Lee would try to monopolise his attention, usually trying to get him involved in an endless computer game. His parents decided to try to help Lee to organize his evenings by using the type of picture timetable that he already had in school. They used symbols and pictures to represent all the things he might want to do and they put self-adhesive Velcro strips on the back. Lee was encouraged to plan his evenings, putting the symbols in a sequence on a long strip of Velcro, which was marked off in quarter-hour sections. The pictures helped him to bring to mind all the options that were available and to make positive choices. A play session with his father was included in the options, but Lee soon learned that this was only available after 8 o'clock (giving his dad time to relax after work.) Because he knew, in advance, that he was going to get time with his dad, he seemed less demanding and anxious about it.

5
Crises: coping with temper tantrums and outbursts

Introduction

This is the only chapter in the book that focuses on a specific type of problem, and it may be useful to explain why. In the long term, temper tantrums and outbursts need to be approached like any of the other problem behaviours mentioned throughout this book. You will need to go through the same process – trying to make sense of the behaviour, thinking in terms of prevention and trying to develop new skills and behaviours. In one sense, a tantrum is just a symptom. It may be a sign that your child is out of his depth, in a situation he has not got the coping skills to deal with. Alternatively, it may show that he does not have the skills to get what he wants in any other way. He may need to learn how to communicate his needs, say 'no' or ask for help. Dealing with these underlying problems is at the heart of prevention and long-term solutions.

Having said this, if you are dealing with temper tantrums and outbursts on a daily basis, you are bound to be looking for short-term strategies, approaches that will help you cope and not make things worse in the long run. It is also important to recognise that, no matter how carefully you plan, no matter how hard you work at prevention, crises will happen. At some stage you are likely to find yourself facing a child who is overwhelmed by anger, frustration or anxiety. You may find yourself in danger of being overwhelmed by exactly the same feelings. You are likely to feel anxious that you are losing control of your child and the situation. It is easy at such times for this to turn to anger or distress. To make matters worse, these situations always seem to happen when there is an audience – whether it is the rest of the class, other members of staff, your partner or everyone who is waiting at the supermarket checkout! In circumstances like these, thinking clearly and acting rationally or reasonably can feel like an impossible challenge. It becomes all too easy to think in terms of winners and losers, to see 'control' as the most important goal and to set unrealistically high standards for yourself and your child.

The focus of this chapter is still very firmly on prevention, but over a much shorter time span. The aim is to help you to prevent difficult situations from turning into disasters and to handle things in a way that does not set up long-term problems. This chapter focuses on ways of responding once the build-up to a tantrum has begun. These strategies may help to head off or defuse a potential crisis – or at least ensure that damage or long-term repercussions are kept to a minimum.

Tantrums and outbursts – keeping the pattern in mind

In Chapter 7, we discuss the meaning of challenging behaviour. We look at the different purposes that the behaviour may serve for your child and the different pay-offs that may ensure the behaviour is repeated. When dealing with tantrums and outbursts – as with any challenging behaviour – it is important to understand the motives and feelings that might be driving what your child is doing. In practical terms, it is especially useful to bear the following in mind:

■ a tantrum may be a sign of 'overload' – that is, rather than being something your child is deliberately choosing to do, it can be an indication that he is experiencing extreme feelings, such as frustration, anxiety or pain
■ tantrums can be 'learned' – your child may have realised that when he throws a tantrum, demands on him are reduced or he gets what he wants.

It is especially important to stop the first sort of tantrum turning into the second. We suggest a range of strategies for dealing with both kinds later in this chapter. When you are deciding which of these to use, it is very helpful to know what kind of tantrum you are dealing with.

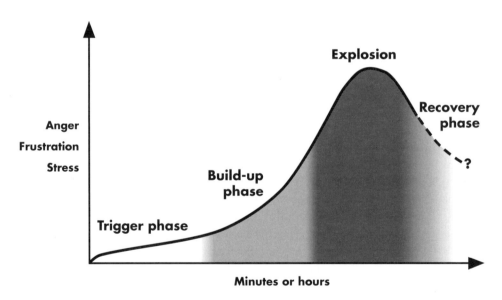

Whatever the reason behind them, tantrums and outbursts tend to follow a similar pattern. The diagram above illustrates the phases that your child may go through as the tantrum develops. The bold line shows the rise in your child's level of anxiety, anger or frustration once something has happened to trigger this build-up. As the level rises further, behaviour is likely to become less and less responsive to your attempts at control. Eventually, he may get past the point of no return, which is where self-control is lost and he is completely swamped by his thoughts and feelings. Your child may then appear to have no awareness of the impact of his actions. He may seem oblivious to most of what you try to say and do. Frequently, this is also where problems of inflexibility become very obvious. Children with autistic spectrum disorders sometimes seem to get locked on to a particular target, which is then pursued with amazing stubbornness.

Of course, the diagram is only an illustration. Inevitably, real life is almost always a lot more complicated and incidents do not happen in nice, tidy stages. Nonetheless, it is especially important to be aware of the following points.

■ You will not always be aware of the trigger. It may be something in the environment that you have not noticed. It could be a thought or a feeling that your child has had.

■ Whether or not a child reacts to a given trigger, and how much effect that trigger has, will vary from day to day.

■ Like all of us, your child may just be reacting to the final straw. Stress levels may have built up over time until it takes just one more thing to trigger a crisis. Often a child may manage to hold things together at school, but go to pieces when he encounters a relatively minor problem at home.

■ Sometimes you may get little or no advance warning. There may be no obvious trigger and there may be no signs of a gradual build-up. The outburst may appear to come from nowhere.

■ At the other extreme, you may get a string of false alarms. This, in itself, can be an indication of tension gradually building up.

Even with all these 'ifs and buts', the diagram of the different phases of a tantrum or outburst does give some useful pointers. You may find that having a plan or a mental map of what is going on actually helps you to feel calmer and more in control. When you are planning what to do or are in the thick of things, it can be helpful to keep this pattern in mind. At different stages, you will need to use different approaches and your priorities and goals are likely to shift as the situation develops.

As you begin to recognise a pattern in your child's behaviour, you may need to plan different approaches for the different phases. In the sections that follow, we suggest a range of tactics, which we have organised in a rough sequence. Based on your knowledge of your child (and what you are trying to achieve), pick one or two strategies to try during each of the main phases. The different phases and the suggested strategies are summarised in the table overleaf. (For anyone interested in a more detailed discussion, we would strongly recommend the book by Dave Hewett which is listed in the Further Reading section.)

Managing tantrums: a summary
of the phases and strategies

Phases	Strategies
Trigger	■ Removing the trigger (or the child) ■ Treating the behaviour as communication ■ Distraction ■ Learning to cope with stress
Build-up	■ Reward reminders ■ Rule reminders ■ Sidestepping 1: opportunities for 'chilling out' ■ Restating your request ■ Side-stepping 2: changing direction ■ Calming things down
Explosion	■ Clearing the decks 1: the environment ■ Clearing the decks 2: other people ■ Getting help ■ A low-key response ■ Intervening physically
Recovery	■ Giving space ■ Getting back to normal ■ Making demands again ■ Talking it through ■ Looking after yourself

The trigger phase: nipping it in the bud

Eventually, you will want your child to be able to cope with some of the things that currently seem to spark off a tantrum. In the short term, however, you will probably want to catch the problem in the early stages and head off a crisis, so let us now look at the strategies listed in the table.

Removing the trigger (or the child)

This will not always be feasible or desirable, but it does make common sense to avoid unnecessary battles. If you cannot do anything about the trigger, it may be possible to move your child out of the situation. Bear the following points in mind.

■ If the tantrum is due to your child being frightened or in pain, it is *essential* to try and deal with the root cause. If your child suddenly starts to have tantrums for no apparent reason, do make sure that you investigate possible medical difficulties.

■ If the trigger is some demand that you are making on your child, you need to be more cautious. Such a trigger might be that you need to say 'no' or ask him to do something he does not want to. You will not want to teach your child to use tantrums as a way of avoiding demands, but you do need to ask yourself the question 'Do I need to be asking my child to do this, in this way, at this moment in time?' It is much easier to change direction (and save face) at this early stage than persist and have to deal with the consequences.

■ If you have tried to teach your child skills for coping with the particular situation, you may want to simply watch and wait. This will give him a chance to try out his new strategies.

Case study

Roshni's teacher used a particular tape to accompany the morning 'hello' time. Roshni began to get in a state at the end of the session and this would sometimes turn into a full-blown tantrum. It wasn't clear what this was about, until the classroom assistant coaxed Roshni into showing her what she wanted. For no reason that anyone could discover, she had become preoccupied with being allowed to turn off the tape recorder when the session finished. She had no way of communicating this and had simply got cross about someone else (her teacher) doing it. As no one else in the group seemed at all interested in this small responsibility, Roshni's teacher decided there was no reason to stop her turning the tape off, if that was what she wanted to do.

An important note: sticking to your guns

If your child is using tantrums to bully you into giving him things or avoid demands, you may want to stick to your guns. This will be especially relevant if you have decided that what you are asking of your child is reasonable and in his long-term best interests. It may be possible to reduce the intensity of the outburst, using some of the suggestions in this and the next section. However, it is vital that you do not give your child whatever he is asking for *during* the tantrum. This is a great deal easier said than done and it requires a lot of determination, especially as, initially, your child's tantrum is likely to get even worse as a result of taking such as step. At the end of Chapter 2 there are some ideas that you may find helpful if you plan to follow this course of action.

Case study

Alistair developed a very strong relationship – bordering on the obsessive – with one of the classroom support assistants. When she gave attention to any other pupil, he would immediately become very agitated and try to grab her hair. Giving him a cuddle would often calm him down, but everyone was worried that this was just feeding his obsession and rewarding his tantrums. Staff finally decided to grasp the nettle. The classroom support assistant deliberately switched her attention from Alistair to other students on a regular, timed basis. At the first sign of aggression directed towards her, she withdrew from the classroom. As far as possible, any tantrum was ignored, but if the well-being of other people in the class was put at risk, the entire class was withdrawn to the library. It was necessary to do this quite often during the first weeks of this strategy and, for obvious reasons, it was extremely disruptive. Over time, however, the frequency and intensity of the outbursts gradually reduced. Other staff made conscious attempts to build relationships with Alistair as well and he had a daily, short, timetabled session with the original assistant.

Treating the behaviour as communication

This means reacting as if your child had been able to say what he did or did not want or tell you how he was feeling. You have to pick up the intention or meaning behind the behaviour and respond accordingly. This may mean letting him have something he wants or allowing him to say 'no' to something he does not want. Here are some points to bear in mind when you apply this strategy.

- You can only do this if you feel it is reasonable to go along with your child's wishes in a given situation. Again, we would stress that it is always worth asking yourself 'Do I really need to say no – is this worth fighting over?' It is sometimes easy to slip into a frame of mind where you feel that you always need to be in control of what your child does and does not do.
- It is essential to use this tactic at the earliest stages of the build-up. If you respond later on, then you are not encouraging communication, you are encouraging tantrums.
- This approach is likely to be most useful with children who have limited communication skills. Ideally you should also be prompting your child to use some other form of communication. For instance, at the first sign of your child getting wound up, you might take him to his communication chart and prompt him to show you what he *does* want.

Case study

Liam was in a specialist unit. It was recognised that, because of major problems with articulation, there was a substantial gap between his understanding and his ability to express himself. With the help of the Picture Exchange Communication System, Liam found it easier to communicate immediate wants and needs. Despite this, there were times when he became agitated, when the communication board just didn't seem to help. Staff decided to provide Liam with a 'moods' page, containing symbols representing three or four basic emotional states. When Liam began to get worked up, they would try to sense his mood, then show him the relevant symbol on the page. Though there was always significant doubt as to whether or not Liam could really differentiate between or identify his own moods, he did start to use the moods page spontaneously. Though staff couldn't always work out why he was pointing to a particular symbol, it did serve to let them know that something was the matter. Sometimes they were able to guess and deal with the problem. At other times, this at least provided them with advance warning, and allowed them to use distractions or activities that soothed him.

Distraction

Once your child has focused on a specific trigger, it may be difficult for him to ignore it. This can apply as much to what he is thinking as to things that are 'out there' in the environment. He may find it hard to shake off a particular thought or give up a plan of action. This may be about something he wants, it could be a particular ritual or pattern that he feels driven to follow or he may be brooding about something that did not happen the way he felt it should. The lack of flexibility, which is such a central part of autism, makes this a particular problem.

When you use distraction, you are trying to interrupt his train of thought, shift his focus of attention or interrupt a pattern. It is usually easiest to do this at an early stage and you need to take account of the following points.

- When you try to distract, you have to be prepared to give up (at least temporarily) any demand that you were making on your child. You may need to come back to it once he has calmed down.
- The distraction will need to be something that really grabs his attention. Sometimes you can use an obsessional interest in this way. Some children respond to a short burst of physical play or a favourite piece of music.
- If your child is experiencing anxiety or uncertainty, it can be helpful to offer an object or an activity that is known to soothe him. This could be a comfort blanket, a special toy or even a quick hand massage.
- If your child only gets attention or fun things to do when someone is trying to distract him from a tantrum, he will quickly learn to throw a tantrum just so he gets these 'goodies'. Make sure that he gets generous amounts of these at other times, without needing to build up towards a tantrum.
- Distraction can also involve briefly removing the child from the situation. This could be a short errand, specially invented for the purpose, or a 'Let's go and look at/for ...'

Case study

Rachel became anxious and agitated whenever she left the house, even though her mum provided her with a picture cue that let her know where she was going. Once she was in this state, she would start pinching her mum's hands and arms, and any attempt to stop this seemed to trigger a major outburst. Rather than wait for the crisis to start, her mum decided to get the distraction in first. Whenever Rachel had to leave the house, she was given her extensive collection of Teletubbies in two shopping bags. These seemed to take her mind off her anxieties and having a bag in each hand made it harder for her to pinch and so start the pattern that usually led to a tantrum.

Case study

Rory was very intolerant of his science teacher's attempts to explain things clearly and simply for the benefit of less able youngsters in the class. If it was obvious to Rory, then it should be obvious to everybody and he should be allowed to get on with the practical work! On occasions, this ended up with Rory charging out of the classroom in a rage or shouting at his teacher. These outbursts were more likely to happen when Rory had had difficulty in a previous lesson or his science work had had to be corrected. The long-term strategy was for Rory to become more aware of the warning signs that he was becoming stressed and to rehearse in his head a 'script' for calming himself down. Progress towards this goal was very limited. In the short term, the classroom support assistant kept a close eye on him and would offer him a book on astronomy (his special interest), whenever she saw trouble brewing. Although this strategy was never openly discussed with Rory, as he was adamant it was the teacher's fault, he did manage to cooperate.

Learning to cope with stress

Youngsters with more sophisticated language skills may progress towards managing their own stress levels. This does seem to be especially hard for many children with autistic spectrum disorders because they may not sense their own moods or have the skills to communicate about them. However, with a lot of adult support, they may learn to spot when they need to ask for help or do something that calms them down.

Getting to this point involves the following strategies.

- The adult will need to monitor the child's mood quite closely, giving feedback that helps the child recognise warning signs in the situation or his own behaviour and feelings.
- Language will need to be very concrete. Words such as 'stress' or 'tense' will need to be translated into actual physical sensations or actions, such as 'when your fists are clenched' or 'when you feel like hitting someone'.
- You need to identify something for your child to do that is likely to make him feel better. Ideally this needs to be something that is easily available and that can be used there and then, in the situation. Some children are able to use books or personal stereos and favourite tapes for this purpose.

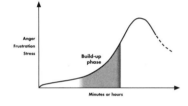

The build-up phase

There is no definite line between the trigger phase and the start of the build-up. Only your detailed knowledge of your child and your reading of the situation will tell you whether or not there is definitely a tantrum on the way. Once you are in this phase, your own anxiety or level of stress may well start to rise (following just the same track as your child's). It is important that your own reactions do not feed your child's agitation. Whatever you are feeling inside, it is always helpful to try and use what is often called a 'low arousal' style:

- deliberately slow yourself down – your thinking, communication and movements
- keep your tone of voice as calm and measured as possible, and language short and simple
- monitor your posture, the expression on your face and where you stand in relation to the child – you want your child to focus on what you are saying so do not let your facial expression or your body language distract or frighten him
- remind yourself of any plan that you have made for dealing with this sort of situation.

In the early part of the build-up phase, you may still be able to regain direct control of your child, even if this means a compromise in terms of what you are expecting him to do. The first three or four strategies suggested below may help. If they do not, and your child becomes more and more wound up, calming your child may become your main priority. The later suggestions may be useful in these circumstances. Try to plan your response, so that you have at least a couple of strategies in mind. Make sure that you have a 'Plan B' to fall back on.

Reward reminders

If tantrums and outbursts are a regular feature of your child's behaviour, you may well have some sort of reward system in place. This will probably be aimed at systematically building up his coping skills or at least encouraging more acceptable behaviour in stressful situations. Even if you are not doing this, your child's activities may be organised so that an enjoyable activity follows a more difficult or demanding one. Now may be the time to jog his memory.

- A brief 'First ..., then ...' prompt may do the trick. You can use it to remind him of the next (and hopefully more enjoyable) activity. You can also use the same phrase as a low-key reminder of any incentive system that is in use.

- You may want to back this up by drawing your child's attention to a picture timetable or a photograph or symbol that shows the reward.
- It is important to avoid getting into a situation where you are trying to tempt (or even bribe) your child into following a request. This is putting too much control in your child's hands. You could inadvertently train him to bully you into giving him rewards.
- Once you have reminded your child, you need to give him time and space – to make sense of what you have said and make up his mind to comply. Avoid the temptation to set a time limit as you may paint him (and yourself) into a corner.

Rule reminders

These may also be useful at an early stage of the build-up phase. They should be done in quite a low-key style, as calmly, simply and briefly as you can manage. As we explained in an earlier chapter, children with autistic spectrum disorders seem to respond best to rules that are fairly impersonal and general. This may be because of their rather rigid style of thinking. It also removes or at least reduces the extra complication of having to deal with a person.

- If your child has a picture timetable, this can be used to get the message across, in the same way that it can be used to remind him about rewards. Drawing attention to a predictable and familiar sequence may also provide him with reassurance.
- It is helpful to have visual reminders of the behaviour that is expected in a particular situation. These can take the form of pictures, cartoons, 'road signs' or even a brief written 'code of conduct'.
- Using these sorts of visual prompts allows you to remind him without needing to use much language or interact in any other way.
- Reminding about rules also includes reminding your child of any punishments that you have decided on in advance.

Side-stepping 1: opportunities for 'chilling out'

With a more able youngster whose behaviour provides early warning signs, it may be possible to organise routines that help him to calm down. This is likely to be particularly useful in the school setting, but it is important to take the following points into consideration.

- Ideally, this needs to be planned with your child's involvement. At the very least it is vital to explain and rehearse what is going to happen.
- It is essential that it is not presented as a form of discipline. The strategy is likely to be much more effective if an adult is seen as someone who is helping your child learn a new skill.
- Getting your child out of the situation probably gives the best chance of interrupting the spiral. Plan and be clear about where he goes, who is responsible and how and when he returns to the situation.
- To begin with, an adult will need to spot the warning signs and prompt your child to leave the situation.
- The strategy is likely to work best if the adult and child have agreed on some sort of private signal or 'code'. If your child fails to cooperate, this at least makes the refusal less of a public challenge to the adult.
- Eventually, some youngsters may be able to identify the warning signs for themselves. They may learn to recognise when they need to get out of the situation.

Case study

Paul was a towering 14-year-old who had learned how intimidating his temper outbursts could be for his mother. These started as spontaneous reactions to his mum's attempts to limit his constant talking about football. There seemed to be a real danger that he would begin to use them whenever he wanted his own way. His mother decided to exploit his interest in football by using the game's own system of warnings. When she saw the early signs, she would show him a yellow card. This was a prompt for Paul to go to his room to calm down and he could earn time watching the sports channel if he complied. Once he had had two warnings (or if the situation suddenly went out of control), he was shown the red card. This meant he had to go to his room for an hour. If he refused to do this, he would lose his TV privileges and his teacher would be told (fortunately, something that he was keen to avoid).

Case study

Jed's difficulties had more to do with anxiety than anger. Having to deal with a range of teachers every day (none of whom really knew him) was one of the hardest parts of the transfer to secondary school. His final year teacher at primary school had been very sensitive to Jed's stress levels. He had known just when to step in and encourage Jed to chill out. The task at secondary school was to help Jed recognise his limits for himself and give him strategies for dealing with his panics. He was given a card to carry in all lessons and if he showed this to staff, he was immediately allowed to leave the lesson, with no questions asked. A form of 'sanctuary' was set up in the Head of Year's office and Jed kept a personal stereo and a tape there. The very fact that he had a way out of difficult situations seemed to be helpful. The only real difficulty was that of persuading him that using the card was not a failure or a defeat. Staff members were encouraged to check periodically to see if he was coping and remind him to use the card if he felt he needed it. Leaving the final decision with him meant that he sometimes misjudged the situation. However, it was felt to be important to encourage him to take on this responsibility.

Restating your request

If none of these approaches have had the effect you want, then you need to make a choice. You can try being even more direct or you can modify what you are asking of your child. However, you can only do the former if your child is still capable of understanding and exercising some degree of self-control. This is the point where you may want to make a final effort to get him to go along with what you have asked. It is especially important to take account of some of the earlier advice about ways of getting your message across.

- Get his attention *before* you start. Getting physically closer to him may help, but be careful. Some children may find this threatening or overstimulating.
- Use a positive instruction. Focus on what you *do* want your child to do rather than on what you do *not* want him to do.
- Be brief and simple – save reasoning and explanation for another time.
- Back up your message with any visual system that is in use.
- Try to keep your style low key and calm, but firm, even though this may be a long way from how you are feeling. It should still sound as if you are making a request rather than giving an order.
- Again, give him time and space to make sense of what you have said and to make up his mind to comply.

Side-stepping 2: changing direction

By this stage, if your child has shown no signs of calming down or going along with your request, it is time to change direction. It is very tempting to match your child's stubbornness with your own. However, unless you have consciously decided that you need to stick to your guns, this is where you need to show some flexibility. It is important not to give in to the temptation of thinking in terms of winners and losers. You need to be looking for ways out of the situation that allow you both to be winners. You might want to consider some of these options.

- Make a different and smaller demand. This could even be something that you know your child is likely to do of his own accord. By taking the initiative and offering an option, you are still staying in overall charge of the situation, but you are also giving your child a way out.
- It may still be worth considering a distraction. All the points raised in the earlier section on distraction still apply.
- Follow your child's lead, either in terms of what he does or says or what he seems to be focusing on. You may see a chance to lead him in a different direction. For instance, if he shows signs of being too hot or thirsty you may want to respond to his needs.

Calming things down

In the later part of the build-up phase, you need to shift your focus. Even if you do not succeed in calming your child down, at least you may be able to stop things getting worse and perhaps prevent your child from completely losing self-control. You may still be able to prevent a minor incident from turning into a major outburst. The tips below may help you.

- At this stage, it is not so much *what* you say as *how* you say it – not just the words you use, but what you say with your tone of voice, expression, position and posture.
- The message you are trying to get across is one of reassurance, that your aim is to help, rather than threaten.
- Everything you do should be slow and calm. Give plenty of space and do not bombard your child with speech or gestures. Try to make what you say and do as simple, repetitive and predictable as possible.
- Do not make new demands. Do not expect, or ask for, a direct response or an answer.
- Leave pauses, where you back off, so that your child does not feel too pressured.

The explosion

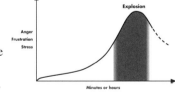

Again, there is no hard and fast rule as to where the last phase ends and this one begins. For some children, it is only a matter of degree. They gradually move beyond any form of influence or persuasion and their behaviour becomes more and more extreme. With other children, there seems to be a point of no return. They may become more and more wound-up during the build-up phase, but then there is a sudden explosion. Often this consists of impulsive and aggressive behaviour that may be directed against other people or things in the immediate environment.

Once matters have reached this stage, the chief priority is to keep the damage to a minimum. This applies to physical damage – whether to the child, other people or the environment – but it is worth stressing that it also applies to psychological damage – to your relationship with your child and your child's dignity. You both have to go on living or dealing with each other once the incident is over. The less ground you have both lost, the better.

During the explosion, think about the applying following strategies.

Clearing the decks 1: the environment

Try to make the environment as safe as possible. If it is feasible, move objects that could be damaged or thrown out of reach.

Clearing the decks 2: other people

Try to get others out of harm's way. This also reduces the chances that your child will be rewarded by the impact that his tantrum is having on others. The attention he gets or the stir that is created may be addictive.

Getting help

You may need to ask for help. If tantrums are a regular feature of your child's behaviour, try to plan how you will deal with them in advance.

- Discuss how you plan to handle the situation with anyone who is likely to be involved.
- It is especially important to be clear about when and how the other person should become involved. Help that is not asked for can simply get in the way or may undermine what you are doing.
- Get agreement about who will call the shots during an incident.

A low-key response

Provided there is no immediate physical danger, it is probably most helpful for adults to keep their distance.

- Continue to use the calming strategies described at the end of the last section.
- The greatest danger is to give in to the temptation to do something when, in fact, doing nothing is the wisest course.

Intervening physically

This is a very difficult decision to make and you always run a significant risk of making matters worse. Though it is possible to offer some very general guidelines, the final judgement will depend on your knowledge of your child and the specific situation. It is important to try and anticipate the likely risks of doing nothing and weigh this against his likely reactions and the related risks if you do intervene physically. School staff will need to ensure that they act in accordance with the school's policies and guidelines on the use of physical intervention. With any pupil who regularly reaches this point, it is essential to plan in detail and liaise closely with the youngster's parents.

There are many more legal restrictions on the actions of adults in schools than there are on parents. Until relatively recently, the legal situation has been very uncertain and teachers have been concerned to avoid the risk of legal challenge. It is especially important for teachers to act in accordance with the following guidelines and these are likely to form a central part of any school policy. Having said this, we do think it is sensible for any parent of a child with an autistic spectrum disorder to take account of them as well.

- As a general rule, do not intervene physically unless you have good reason to think that there is an immediate danger of significant injury to your child or others or if there may be serious damage to property.
- Wherever possible, try to contain the situation using other methods before you resort to using physical intervention.
- The aim of any physical intervention should be to ensure physical safety – not to physically punish or cause pain. Members of staff in schools are forbidden to use physical punishment by law.
- For this reason, the amount of physical force that is used should be the minimum needed to achieve the goal of safety and it must be in proportion to the risks and the severity of the incident.
- If at all possible, continue to try and calm the child at the same time. Use physical force for the least time possible and give your child the chance to show that he has managed to regain self-control.

Afterwards – the recovery phase

You may have managed to head off an outright explosion or the worst may seem to be over. Unfortunately, there is no guarantee that things will get back to normal straight away. Your child may continue to be in a state of stress for some time, with any small thing triggering a further explosion. This is especially likely if you have been unable (or have chosen not) to do anything about the original trigger. To give your child the best chance of calming right down, we would suggest taking the following steps.

Giving space

The commonest mistake is to move in too quickly, whether this is to tell the child off, sort out the damage or put the child back in the situation that triggered the tantrum. Your natural instinct may well be to punish or communicate your disapproval in some way. You are also still likely to be feeling fairly stressed yourself. Giving your child space gives him a chance to calm down and you a chance to regain your own self-control and powers of judgement.

Getting back to normal

After a major tantrum, your child may well continue to feel highly anxious. Some children are frightened by feeling so far out of their own (and other people's) control. Children who are more socially aware may fear the damage they have done to their relationship with the adult. These are all good reasons for trying to reintroduce at least a degree of structure, order and predictability into the situation as soon as you can. Whatever systems were routinely in place need to be reactivated. Another important part of getting back to normal is to rebuild bridges between the adult and the child. Finding something that the child can do, and which you will be able to praise, can be a helpful tactic.

Making demands again

This is one of the toughest dilemmas to deal with, particularly if you feel your child has been using tantrums to avoid doing what you want him to. You do not want to trigger a further tantrum, but you do not want to teach your child that tantrums work. Depending on the issue at stake, it may be necessary to reimpose the demand. If you have to do this, think about the following:

- waiting until your child has calmed down
- scaling down your demand and settling for some degree of compromise
- making it easier for your child to go along with your request – you may want to increase any incentives or at least ensure that some less stressful activity follows whatever it is that you want your child to do.

Talking it through

It can be helpful for older children with better language skills to talk through the incident. Careful judgement is needed because some children seem especially prone to relive events once they begin to recall them. On occasions, the emotions this arouses can then be more extreme than those experienced in the original situation. However, this sort of debriefing can give you useful information on how your child experienced the situation, which can help in preventing a repetition in future. You may also be able to use this sort of session to increase your child's awareness of his own and other people's feelings and help him take more responsibility for self-control. If you do try this, you need to be aware of the following points:

- try to avoid blame or attempt to secure promises about future behaviour
- focus on the 'facts', as your child saw them – especially what he understood about other people's involvement in the situation
- try to find something he did right or tried to do right
- look for one small thing he could have done differently – try to find out if your child has managed to cope more successfully with a similar situation and focus on what he did that helped in this success.

Getting support

Dealing with major outbursts and tantrums can be exceptionally stressful, particularly if things have not gone according to plan. It is important to be aware of your own physical and emotional state, to try to take care of your own needs and to find the support you need to do so. Whether or not this is possible, and how it is done, will depend a great deal on your circumstances. Schools should consider how they can offer staff the opportunity to debrief. At the very least, it is important for someone to check how the person involved with the incident is feeling. This sort of support can be much more difficult for parents to obtain. Partners may be helpful, but some parents rely on friends or informal support networks (often consisting of other parents of children with autistic spectrum disorders). Above all, it is essential that you do not underestimate your own need for emotional support. Look at again at the points made at the end of Chapter 2.

Case study

Tony was a 12-year-old with severe learning difficulties and very limited communication skills. He was having regular tantrums at transition points during the school day. Staff used a combination of the approaches described in this and earlier chapters. Pictures were used to give Tony clear advance warnings of any changes and, if he had to move between classrooms, he was allowed to go ahead of everyone. He took a favourite cushion and a bag of 'twiddlers' with him and if he showed signs of agitation, he was encouraged to sit on the cushion and play with the contents of the bag. Once staff judged he was calm (and this could take as long as ten minutes), he was invited to join the class and every effort was made to make this as rewarding as possible. If there were further outbursts, he was redirected to his cushion, but was only allowed access to his toys once he had calmed down.

6
Helping your child to cope with change

Introduction

The emphasis so far has mainly been on preventing challenging behaviour by adapting the environment to 'fit' your child. The aim has been to accommodate at least some of the difficulties that are part of his autism. In particular, we have emphasised the need for structure and routine. As well as helping to communicate our expectations, these also offer a way of accommodating the need for sameness and lack of flexibility that are core features of all autistic spectrum disorders.

However, children with these difficulties also need help to learn how to fit (as far as possible) into our world – the environment of the family, school and community. Change is a part of that world. Helping your child to tolerate change is one of the most important targets that you can work towards. Before looking at the various techniques that you can use, it is useful to think about the different aspects of the problem.

- Your child may find it hard to tolerate change in the ways things are done or the order in which they happen.
- He may have a strong need for his physical environment to be arranged in a certain way or remain constant.
- As well as imposing a particular template on the environment, children with autistic spectrum disorders may also impose patterns on their own behaviour. Obsessions and rituals provide predictability and help protect the individual from the demands of their environment. Difficulties often occur when there is a need for the person to change or limit the behaviour and patterns that are connected to these obsessions and rituals.

Just as with other aspects of the triad of impairments, it is important to emphasise that individual children will vary greatly in their tolerance of change. However, changes to familiar routines, interruptions to rituals and repetitive patterns of behaviour or encounters with feared aspects of the environment can all be very powerful triggers for challenging behaviour. Just as importantly, these problems can also be very serious obstacles to learning new skills and behaviours. For both reasons, then, it is essential to work towards increasing your child's flexibility while at the same time recognising that this may well be a major challenge for both of you.

Though it may sound like a contradiction in terms, a structured approach to the introduction of change is at the core of the approaches that are outlined below. Changes need to be planned for and you must plan to introduce change and increase flexibility.

Planning for change – some general guidelines

However carefully you have tried to structure your child's environment, unplanned changes are bound to happen. These events – and your child's reactions to them – may help to give you an idea of just how sensitive to and aware your child is of change. At this point, it may also be worth emphasising that, just because a child seems to cope with a major change, such as a move of house or a foreign holiday, it does not mean that he will be able to cope with apparently much smaller changes in his routine or environment. New carpets, rearranged furniture or a different route to the shops may be much harder to deal with. It is as if, in the case of really major changes, your child has no pattern or template against which to compare them. When the change is on a much smaller scale, and is in the context of a lot that is familiar, he has lots of points of reference and comparison. He can actually see and measure the differences.

Because change is inevitable (and desirable) you need to prepare and plan for it, from the very beginning. It is useful to think in terms of the following general guidelines.

- **Plan for changes that can be anticipated** Some changes can be anticipated well ahead – changes of school or class teacher are obvious examples. The sections that follow outline a variety of ways in which to prepare your child so he can cope with these.

Case study

Jason had already had major difficulties with the transition from playgroup to the local nursery. His mother was concerned about how he would handle the much bigger change he would experience when he moved into the reception class of the local primary. She decided to use his fascination with videos, making a video of his new classroom and some of the key activities of the school day. She included things that were likely to be 'constants', but also included clips recorded on different days. This helped reduce the risk that his expectations would become too fixed. He watched this time after time, and showed very few signs of anxiety, once the 'big day' arrived.

- **Introduce planned changes to routines** Even if there is no immediate need for change, it is important to work towards greater flexibility by gradually introducing minor changes. It is especially important to prevent your child getting too attached to the patterns and routines that you have devised, in order to structure his environment. Do not let a framework become a cage.
- **Give advance warning of changes that can be anticipated** This applies to any departure from familiar routines. However, do not forget that some children will need to be warned of the change from one activity to another, even when the overall routine is familiar and consistent.
- **Make planned changes a small step at a time** Whether you are trying to impose limits on obsessions or rituals, vary the routine of the day or deal with a particular fear, it is usually most effective to introduce the change a small step at a time.

Case study

Aran's mum was feeling claustrophobic about his determination to sit as close to her as physically possible at mealtimes. To resolve this difficulty, his parents used his rigidity to their own advantage. They taught him to make sure that his chair was always carefully located on a special square of carpet. Once he had become hooked on this arrangement, the square was moved away from his mother's place, a short distance at a time.

- **Be alert to new obsessions and rituals** In Pat Howlin's words, 'prevention is better than late intervention'. She emphasises the importance of watching out for children developing new obsessions and rituals. Though some may just be passing phases and some may seem quite harmless, she stresses the importance of trying to anticipate and deal with those that may become a problem in later life. She emphasises particularly the need to think about how any given behaviour will be viewed by others as the child gets older.
- **Try to stay in control of obsessions and rituals** This does not mean trying to prevent them entirely, but it does mean trying to set limits on where, when and for how long your child engages in them.

Case study

Sideeq was in his final year at a village primary school. His parents and teacher had serious misgivings about how he would cope with the move to the large secondary school in a nearby market town. A 'Circle of Friends' was established, consisting of children who would be moving up with Sideeq, and they joined him in a number of introductory visits to the school. The first of these took place after the school day had ended, when the building was empty of pupils. The next two were timed so that lessons were in progress. Then, finally, the group spent a full morning experiencing the bustle of transitions between lessons. Sideeq managed to cope with the normal transition visits with the rest of his class and there were no major difficulties at the beginning of the new school year.

Case study

Emily could not tolerate the smallest change in her physical environment. Everything had to be 'just so' and for six years the furniture had been arranged in exactly the same way. Her parents began to feel like they were prisoners in their own home and finally decided to do something about it. They had a new carpet laid and then had the old one put back on top. A small strip at a time, they removed pieces of the old carpet, gradually revealing the new one. Once Emily had got used to this, they set about varying the layout of the furniture. They used tape to mark an outline round the settee and explained to Emily that the settee had to be inside these limits (an idea that immediately appealed to her very tidy mind). A small distance at a time, her parents moved the tape, enlarging the area in which the settee was located (making sure that they kept repositioning it within this space). Eventually, they were able to abandon the tape and Emily seemed to become more relaxed about these sorts of changes.

Giving advance warnings of change

Even when the overall sequence of events is familiar and consistent, some children find it hard to cope with the transition from one activity to the next. Giving some sort of advance notice or warning can be extremely helpful in reducing adverse reactions (although it needs to be pointed out that there seems to be a small proportion of children who fret and worry if given too much notice of an impending change). Many of the suggestions given in Chapter 4 about routines and timetables are helpful precisely because they offer advance notice of change to the child. The degree of sophistication that is needed in any advance warning will depend on your child's level of understanding and on how inflexible he is. Here are some strategies to consider.

- **Mark endings** With younger children and those whose understanding is limited, it is very helpful to have some way of clearly signalling that an activity is ending and that something different is about to begin. At the very least, try to use a gesture that stands for 'finished', say it as well and have a clear pack away routine.
- **Use additional cues to mark transitions** In some classrooms, special music is used to signal endings and transitions. This gives an additional and extended cue (in case the child fails to take in the original warning). It also gives advance notice that the ending is imminent and this may make it easier for the child to give up a favourite activity. Visual systems, such as sand-timers, can also be used and clockwork ringing timers provide both visual and auditory cues that the ending is coming up.
- **'And now ...'** In addition to letting your child know that an activity is ending, we have also stressed the importance of letting him know what is coming next. If he is operating within a routine, then past experience will help him to do this. In Chapter 4 you will recall we described in detail how to use photographs and symbols to build up your child's ability to predict events. Even if your child can only make sense of a single photograph at a time, this can still be extremely helpful in reducing anxiety and uncertainty regarding what might be about to happen.
- **'First ..., then ... and then ...'** Again, it can be very helpful to work on your child's ability to use a visual timetable. This can help him to anticipate and master the planned and foreseeable changes in daily routines.
- **Build up tolerance of uncertainty** The obvious danger with any routine is that your child will become hooked on it. There are various ways in which you can increase your child's tolerance of uncertainty, and picture timetables are especially useful in this regard. Even if the events on the timetable change, the fact that the timetable is always there provides reassurance. Here are some tips on how to introduce change.
  - Introduce small changes to the sequence of events, explaining this by changing the order of pictures on the timetable.
  - Once a child has got used to reading timetables, you may want to negotiate the sequence of events from a given range of activities, immediately before the morning or afternoon begins. In effect, you are reducing the amount of advance warning that is provided.
  - For children with relatively good levels of understanding, it is sometimes possible to help them anticipate and deal with a degree of uncertainty. This can be done by actually telling them that, at a certain time, there will be a surprise activity. They will know when it is going to happen, but not what. The surprise slot can even be shown on the timetable by a blank card or question mark.
  - A 'social story' can also be used to help your child anticipate his own reactions (and know that other people may also feel nervous) and provide him with suggestions for coping. These will need to include phrases that your child can use to reassure himself and act as prompts to any relaxation routine that you may have taught.

Jitesh's picture timetable for shopping expeditions was mentioned in Chapter 4. His mum managed to extend the number of shops he would visit by adding them on to the established sequence, but he would not tolerate any change in the familiar order. She decided to vary the order of the final two shops, letting Jitesh know just before they set off. Although he protested at first, he gradually got used to the uncertainty. It was then possible to vary the order of the last three, then four and so on.

Having a detailed daily timetable had helped Chris adapt to the more complex organisation of a Year 6 class, but he had become overly dependent on the routine. He had particular difficulty either when a supply teacher took his class or when a particular topic or subject was taught by one of the other Year 6 staff. The names of all the staff who taught his class (and of the supply teachers who were most commonly employed) were put on individual cards and these were 'posted' on the relevant parts of Chris' individual timetable at the start of the day. As a longer-term strategy to build up his flexibility, one timetable slot (per week initially, then per day) was replaced with a picture of his teacher. This signified that Chris had to go to his teacher to find out what he was to do. Initially he was offered two or three options, which always included something that he enjoyed. Gradually these were made more formal and demanding.

A small steps approach to change

However careful you are to introduce deliberate changes and to build up your child's overall tolerance of change, there will come a time when you realise that your child has become hooked on a particular routine or pattern. This might be to do with following a certain sequence, demanding that part of the physical environment is 'just so' or doing things only in a certain way. Some children with autistic spectrum disorders can react with real distress or anger if the certainty of these familiar patterns is challenged in any way. It is important to appreciate that this is considerably more than just protest about not being able to have their own way. For many, the degree of distress seems much more acute than it might be if they had, for instance, experienced some sort of physical injury.

To tackle these difficulties, very careful and detailed planning is needed. Some of the case studies in this chapter have already illustrated a golden rule:

Always introduce any change in very, very small steps, focusing on one aspect of the situation at a time.

This general approach is particularly helpful when trying to tackle the problems with eating and toileting that are quite common in youngsters with autistic spectrum disorders. Many of them are related to wider difficulties in terms of rigidity – the need to do things in a particular way or for aspects of the environment to be just so.

Problems with eating

Very rigid and restricted food preferences are especially common and a significant cause of worry or distress for many parents. The problem may be that the child will only eat one or two types of food or will only tolerate a particular brand (for instance, only chocolate buttons with the Cadbury's logo). Sometimes it is the consistency of the food that is the problem, with a dislike of sauces and 'messy' food being quite common, or, at the opposite extreme, a total intolerance of lumps. Occasionally, children will become fixated on only eating food of a particular colour. You may find some of the guidelines below helpful in these situations.

- **'First ..., then ...'** Offer a very small amount of new food and immediately follow it with a mouthful of the favourite. It can be helpful to have the two types of food in separate bowls. Following the principle of visual systems, one family used a tray that was originally intended for making ice cubes, with alternating portions of the new food and the old favourite.
- **Vary one thing at a time** Try to find out if your child is especially hooked on one particular aspect of his favourite food – the texture, colour or shape of it, for example. Some parents have had to resort to slowly introducing food dyes or building up the consistency of foods by gradually reducing the extent of the liquidizing.
- **Start with the smallest possible change** Whatever change you do make, keep the steps as small as possible. In a similar way, expect only the smallest change from your child. To start with, it may be enough for him to tolerate just having a small quantity of the new food on his plate. The next step might be to have the new food touch his lips, but without any expectation that it be swallowed or tasted.
- **Try a little with a lot** Sometimes children will try a small amount of a new food if it is presented mixed in with a familiar favourite, though some children seem to have almost telepathic powers when it comes to detecting new food that has been disguised in this way!
- **Keep the pressure off** This is one of the easiest pieces of advice to give, but one of the hardest to follow. It is exceptionally easy to become anxious about your child's diet and this tension can easily be communicated. Offer the food and then try to stand back – mentally and, if need be, physically. Some parents have found it helpful to offer a low-key reward when the child is eating – playing a favourite tape, putting the TV on or simply chatting (provided this does not actually distract). When your child stops eating, the tape or TV can be turned off (again, in a low-key way).
- **Take stock of your child's diet** If you have any reason to think that your child's diet is inadequate in its quantity or range, try to take stock of exactly what he eats over a two- or three-day period. Do not forget to include snacks between meals and check what is happening at school. Sometimes there are surprising inconsistencies or at least clues about what new food to try next. Often parents are surprised by just how much their child is eating, but if concerns remain, then consult your family doctor, who may want to refer you to a dietitian.

Case study

At the age of seven, John was firmly entrenched in a pattern of only eating chips, chocolate and biscuits. His increasing weight was posing medical and management difficulties. He had just entered a phase of imitating his older brother and his parents decided to try and turn this to their advantage. The brothers were seated opposite each other and each was given a small helping of John's favourite food. John was encouraged to look at and copy his brother as they each ate several small portions of the favourite. Once John was clearly aware of, and enjoying, this game, tiny amounts of unfamiliar food were introduced between the helpings of the favourites. The quantities and the range were built up gradually until John was eating a better, more balanced diet. The range remained somewhat restricted, but his parents felt that this was a fair compromise.

Case study

Staff at Peter's school for children with severe learning disabilities were not sure whether his behaviour at lunchtimes was the result of rigidity or not. He seemed to have got into a pattern of eating one or two mouthfuls, then getting out of his seat and hovering nearby. After a lot of coaxing and nagging, he would be back for another couple of mouthfuls and then be off again. He seemed quite happy with the food that was on offer and did not seem to have a problem about being in the dining hall, which was the staff's other hunch. In the end, staff decided to treat his behaviour as an indication that he had finished. Staff did not react when he got out of his seat, but, if he had not returned after a minute, they would say clearly and loudly, 'Peter's finished' and start to clear his plate. This produced a very rapid return to the table so staff began to reduce the time before they started to remove his plate. They did this gradually, in case Peter actually needed to have a short time out away from the group table. In the event, he quickly learned to sit for the whole meal. The behaviour seemed to have been a habit that, perhaps, was strengthened by the attention and interaction it created.

Problems with toileting

Even when children have become aware of their bodily functions and are showing signs of being able to exercise some degree of control, problems about where and how they choose to perform are common. Frequently, the problem is the result of inflexibility. It is as if the child has got stuck in an earlier stage or routine. Sometimes there may also be a significant element of fear. A very common example is that of the child who will only poo when put in a nappy (even though he very clearly has the self-control to hold on until the nappy is available). As well as being very inconvenient, this can be extremely frustrating. Even when children have all the necessary skills and self-control, they may not be aware of or concerned about social norms and other people's expectations.

Toileting problems often take a long time to resolve, but it is important to remember that usually things do improve, often out of the blue. As with food problems, it is useful to adopt a small steps approach. It is also important, though, to take account of other aspects of your child's difficulties. You may find these tips helpful.

- **Think about whether *you* are ready** One parent, who succeeded in sorting out her child's toilet training, compared it to giving up smoking or going on a diet. It requires that kind of determination and commitment. You have to be prepared for setbacks and you will need to persist. You have to decide whether or not it really is a priority and if now is the time to tackle it.
- **Avoid starting too early** Starting before your child is ready may well create stress for you and him – and stress may well increase rigidity. Look for these signs of readiness (but also consider using a timed toileting schedule if these are still not evident by the time your child is six or so).
  - Can he remain dry or unsoiled for one or two hours at a time?
  - Does he notice when he is wet or soiled?
  - Does he seem to be aware when performing?
  - Are there any signs of awareness or interest in the toilet and what happens there?
  - Is there any pattern to wetting or soiling?
- **Develop a clear, consistent routine** Include visits to the toilet in your child's daily schedule (preferably at times when he is likeliest to go) and show this in any picture

timetable system that you have managed to establish. Consistently use a clear routine for each of the steps involved in going to the toilet.

- **Make sure that expectations are clear** Try to use visual cues that remind your child of the behaviour expected at each step (including remaining on the toilet until fully finished). This may mean drawing some fairly explicit cartoons! With some children you may also be able to use a social story to help them learn the sequence. Boys sometimes seem to learn by imitating their father or brother.

- **Getting used to the bathroom** It is important that your child is relaxed about being in the bathroom. You may need to use a small steps approach to build up the time he spends in the bathroom or even to get him to go near the doorway. Provide low-key activities that are pleasant and calming – you want your child to relax but not be too distracted. You need to build up positive associations with being in the bathroom.

- **Getting used to sitting on the toilet** Once your child is used to the bathroom, you may still need to use small steps – moving from sitting on a potty in the bathroom, through a potty chair to a seat on the toilet itself. Providing some form of footrest, or even a clip-on table, may help your child to feel more secure. You may even have to start by having your child sit on your lap while you sit on the toilet. Try to gradually extend the time on the toilet, keeping your child relaxed.

- **Giving up nappies** It is quite common for children to get into a pattern of only being able to wee or poo when actually wearing a nappy and waiting until the nappy is put on before doing so. There are several strategies that may help.
  - Try to restrict use of the nappy to the bathroom. If your child waits until you put a nappy on him before performing, then put it on in the bathroom. Otherwise, take your child to the bathroom if there is any sign of him performing.
  - If he does soil the nappy, demonstrate where you expect the contents to go by emptying it down the toilet.
  - If he still will not perform without the nappy but will sit on the toilet, encourage him to use the nappy while he is sitting on the toilet.
  - If you can establish this pattern, try cutting progressively bigger and bigger holes in the nappy, so that he ends up performing in the toilet.

Case study

Simon's teachers were trying to get him ready to transfer to a mainstream primary school for the beginning of Year 4. They were worried that his insistence on sitting down to wee would result in adverse comment from other boys. The first step in getting him to use a urinal was to teach him to stand up to wee in the toilet at home. His father modelled the necessary behaviour. His teacher also suggested putting a ping-pong ball down the toilet to encourage an accurate aim and provide a motivator – something that had worked well for another child in the same unit. In fact, this was not needed and actually created difficulties – Simon was so tidy minded that he insisted it be removed immediately!

Case study

Brian was a very rigid ten-year-old who insisted that his father put a nappy on him whenever he needed to wee. Every trick in the book had been tried, but the most that had been achieved was getting Brian to go into the toilet for the nappy to be put on. In desperation, the next time Brian showed he needed to wee, his father took him into the toilet but then refused to put the nappy on him (or let him out of the toilet). When Brian was clearly desperate, his father prompted him to sit on the toilet and used the running tap trick. Although Brian put up a good deal of protest, he finally did wee on the toilet and appeared to make the connection between this and his dad's enthusiastic praise.

Aisha had responded well to a simple picture timetable that included a timed routine for visits to the toilet. Staff always prompted her to take the relevant picture to the next activity (including the toilet). Aisha had already started to anticipate some transitions by going and to fetch the relevant picture, and this started to happen with the visit to the toilet before dinner. One day, she took the toilet picture ahead of its usual place in the routine. Just in case, staff took her to the toilet and realised that Aisha had clearly communicated an urgent need to go.

Jamie seemed to be terrified by the toilet (especially if he was anywhere near the bathroom when it flushed). His parents used an approach that they came across in very helpful American book by Maria Wheeler (details of which are given in the Further Reading section). They drew a picture of Jamie standing next to the toilet to show what they were expecting. They put favourite pictures on the walls and played his Thomas the Tank Engine story tape. They encouraged Jamie to stand on a favourite rug that was placed in the doorway of the bathroom, gradually building up the time, using a ringing timer. As soon as the timer went off, Jamie was given a chocolate button and shown the cartoon picture. In very small steps, the rug was moved nearer and nearer to the toilet, the time was built up and Jamie was encouraged to look at a favourite book. After four weeks, he was actually sitting on the toilet. The time was gradually extended until his parents were able to establish a timed toileting schedule.

Obsessions, rituals and repetitive behaviours

The obsessions, rituals and repetitive behaviour that are common in people with autistic spectrum disorders can take many forms. They can range from a fascination with trying to make everything spin to compulsively questioning other people about the colour, make, model and mileage of their car. Although no one fully understands why these types of behaviour are so common, they are generally thought of as instances of the need for sameness.

As we mentioned in the guidelines for planning for change at the beginning of this chapter, it is important to try and establish some sort of control over these behaviours. They may cut the child off from other experiences and opportunities to learn and, if interrupted, the child's reactions of distress and protest may cause serious difficulties. Again, we should stress that, usually, the aim is not to try and eliminate the repetitive behaviours altogether. In the long term, our aims should be to reduce the stress that seems to drive these behaviours and give children better ways of occupying themselves and dealing with anxiety. Small steps approaches to change are a basic ingredient in dealing with many obsessional and repetitive behaviours. Here are some of the most useful strategies for dealing with these difficulties.

- **Rationing the objects** If the problem involves particular objects (for instance, twiddling sticks or spinning things), it can be helpful to try to ration your child's access to them. To do this you may need to:
  - encourage your child to focus on just one special object or a small collection of them – having a box of 'super-twiddlers', for example

- redirect your child to the box or to the special twiddler if he tries to twiddle any other object
- try to *gradually* reduce the time that a specific set of objects or a particular thing your child is hooked on is available to him
- set limits and gradually reduce them if large collections or lining-up rituals become a problem – the limits being framed in terms of the numbers of items involved or the amount of space that they can occupy.

Case study

Left to his own devices, Sam would spend hours flapping sticks, rulers, crayons and so on close to the corner of his eye. This behaviour was seriously interfering with his ability to undertake any tasks independently or to learn to play in a more constructive way. His teacher built up a small collection of 'super-flappers' – items that seemed to work especially well when flapped and that he seemed especially attracted to. These were stored in a box and it was kept in one particular corner of the classroom. Whenever Sam began to flap, the object was taken away from him, he was redirected to the special box and encouraged to flap only with the items in the box. A specific 'flapping time' was also included in each third of his school day. Once Sam was spontaneously going to his corner to flap, periods of time when the box was not accessible were gradually introduced and extended. If he flapped any other object at any other time or if he went in search of the box, he would be shown his picture timetable and told, 'First ..., then flapping'. As a longer-term aim, the school also worked on his ability to play with action toys in a more appropriate way. Various forms of marble run were chosen because they incorporated the sort of visual pay-off that Sam seemed to enjoy.

- **Rationing the place** A variation on the same theme is to try and restrict the activity to just one place (preferably marked out with some form of clearly visible boundary) or to particular rooms in the house. This becomes the special place for the special activity. Your child is then encouraged to go there whenever he engages in his particular interest, but then access to that place or room is gradually restricted.
- **Rationing the time** It may be impossible to clear the environment of all the objects that your child might be able to use in his obsessions. Equally, the problem may be that he insists on talking about a particular topic continually. Aim to gradually build up blocks of time when the special activity or interest is actively discouraged. Try the following:
  - use 'first ..., then ...' statements, with pictures if possible
  - use a kitchen timer to set limits to rituals, then gradually reduce the time allowed for them
  - make a cardboard clock, set the hands to the time that the special activity will be allowed, then fix this next to the real clock.

Case study

Hannah was coping well in a mainstream class of nine- and ten-year-olds and she usually seemed quite happy. Her teacher was a bit concerned about her tendency to always steer conversations towards her favourite topic – animals. They also tended to pop up in her written work. Other children were well aware of this and were beginning to find it a bit of a strain on their otherwise generally positive relationships with her. Hannah's tendency to go on in this way did not seem to be a sign of anxiety, but she did

A small steps approach is one of the most important strategies to use in situations such as this. The following strategies may help to reduce your child's fear. It is also sensible to use some of these strategies if you are having to introduce your child to an experience or situation that you know may frighten him.

- **Identify the source of the fear** This may require quite a lot of trial and error and sometimes children develop associations with the *situation* where something frightening has happened. This means that the situation itself triggers the fear even if the original cause is no longer part of it.
- **Provide reassurance** Your child needs to be confident that you are not going to suddenly put him in a situation that he cannot handle. Initially, you may need to avoid the situation and offer lots of reassurance. Even with children who have the necessary understanding, attempts to reason the child out of his fear are unlikely to be successful. It is interesting to note that this tends also not to work with the phobias of people who do not have autistic spectrum disorders.
- **Plan a sequence of small steps** Try to work out a sequence of small steps or stages that will gradually expose your child to the situation or experience that is triggering the fear. You might want to think in terms of:
  - reducing the physical distance – finding ways to get your child closer and closer to whatever he is afraid of
  - extending the time – exposing your child to the source of his fear for progressively longer periods of time
  - moving from pretend to real – using drawings, pictures, toys and videos to get your child used to the real thing, gradually increasing how realistically the situation or object is portrayed
  - modifying the situation so that your child has to deal with only one small aspect at a time – for example, getting used to sitting in the dentist's chair, it tilting back, having the light on, the noise of the drill and so on – all as separate steps.

Case study

Robbie totally refused to go into the hall for assembly and the problem seemed to be fear of the large space, combined with the crowding. The first step in conquering this fear was to coax him into the hall when nobody else was there. He was simply asked to 'Come and look.' To begin with, he was hardly expected to set a foot in the hall, nor stay for any length of time. Once he did, an activity that he liked was always made available when he went into the hall. Once he was able to spend five minutes in the hall, he was gradually coaxed closer and closer, for longer and longer, when the hall was full of children. This started with just glancing through the window, moved to him standing in the doorway, then on to him looking at a favourite book in the hall and, finally, to him joining his class for assembly.

Case study

Pat Howlin quotes a very helpful example of a child with a phobia of baths who would only be washed in the sink or a baby bath. His parents let him get used to a new bath that was to be installed by using it as a toy store. Then he was washed while standing fully clothed in the empty bath. His parents then progressed to washing him in a washing-up bowl, placed inside the bath. This was followed by them gradually raising the water level in the actual bath while still washing him in the washing-up bowl. Finally, they removed the bowl and extended his time in the bath.

- **Let your child set the pace** It is important to raise demands gradually. You will need to exert some pressure. However, this needs to be gentle and you will need to back off if your child becomes too distressed. Getting the balance right can be difficult, and any step forward may initially cause your child a degree of anxiety.
- **Build up positive associations** Before you expose your child to any step, it can be helpful to involve him in an activity that he finds pleasurable or relaxing. Sometimes it is also possible to continue this while he copes with the situation.
- **Use a Social Story to explain** Sometimes children are frightened of things because they do not understand them. A Social Story can be used to explain the situation or the event or at least to make it more familiar and predictable. Opportunities to read through the story with a familiar adult in a relaxed setting can help desensitise the child to his fear.

Case study

Jeet had always been quite happy walking to the shops until, one day, he was badly scared by the sound of a motorbike being revved up. After that, he seemed to be terrified of all traffic noise and would not go anywhere near the main road. His dad dealt with the problem by taking him out on walks in the neighbourhood, planning these so they got progressively longer and gradually took in busier and busier streets. While out on these walks, Jeet was fed with a steady supply of sweets. Eventually, Jeet could cope with standing in a side street, looking at the busy main road. He gradually stood for longer and got closer until he was once again coping with short walks along the main road. Although he was obviously still nervous, he no longer panicked and dropped to the ground.

Case study

For no reason that anyone could work out, Ellie suddenly developed what seemed like a phobia about wearing shoes and even reacted to the sight of them. Her parents set up sessions where she was given spoonfuls of her favourite ice-cream while a pair of glittery, open-toed sandals were put gradually closer and closer to her feet. Eventually, she was able to tolerate them touching her feet and they were put on the tips of her toes for gradually longer periods of time. Once she would tolerate wearing them for a while, the whole process was repeated with her shoes.

7
New ways of behaving – replacing old problems with new skills

Introduction

When we think of challenging behaviour, we tend to think in terms of what the child does and, usually, what he does too much of – he hits, has a tantrum, runs away, disturbs others. When we start planning what to do, the natural tendency is to focus on what we want the child to *stop* doing or at least do less of. In turn, this can lead to us putting most of our efforts into finding ways to discourage the particular problem behaviour. Unless we also think about skills and behaviour that we want to teach or encourage – things we want our child to *start* doing – we may end up creating a number of significant practical problems for ourselves and our child. These problems include the following.

■ **Letting your child know what you do *not* want him to do may not provide him with many clues about what you *do* want him to do** It may seem very obvious, but remember that even very able youngsters with autistic spectrum disorders have problems with making sense of other people's intentions and motives. It is almost always necessary to spell things out in a great deal more detail than you normally would. This means being clear about the behaviour you are aiming to discourage *and* the behaviour you want to put in its place.

■ **Your child may not know how to behave differently** Although you may have managed to make it clear what you do want, it does not mean that your child will necessarily have the skills to behave in this way. For a child with an autistic spectrum disorder good behaviour may actually be harder to learn than problem behaviour. It requires many skills and sensitivities in just those areas of development that are affected by the core impairments.

■ **Old problems may just be replaced with new ones aimed at achieving the same purpose or getting the same pay-off** Most challenging behaviour has some sort of pay-off or is done for a particular purpose. If we forget to teach our child better ways to get these pay-offs, then he may simply discover some new sort of problem behaviour to achieve the same results. A youngster called Owen provided a graphic example of this trap. Because of concerns about his physical well-being, his teachers made a very determined and successful effort to stop his headbanging. Unfortunately, as the headbanging declined, he started to hit out at staff. The problem only improved when he was provided with an alternative system for communicating his needs. Headbanging, then hitting, had been his only ways of showing that something was wrong or that he wanted something.

These are all reasons for it being necessary to think in terms of *replacing* rather than just stopping challenging behaviour. Remember that there is no such thing as 'non-behaviour' – children have to do something. In any long-term plan, it is therefore essential to think about teaching or encouraging new skills and behaviours chosen specifically to reduce your child's need for his challenging behaviour. The questions you asked in Step 7 of the Eight-step Plan in Chapter 2 are designed to help you identify what new skills and behaviour to target. Your answers to these questions will depend, to a considerable extent, on the conclusions you drew when thinking about Step 5 – when you thought about the purpose and meaning of your child's behaviour. This is a topic that we now need to consider in more detail.

Thinking about the meaning of behaviour

Unfortunately, there is no simple or sure way to work out the meaning or purpose of a particular behaviour. The same behaviour can serve a number of different functions or achieve a range of different pay-offs depending on the child and the situation. For instance, one child may question repetitively about future events because he feels worried and unsure about what is going to happen when. He wants the certainty and predictability that comes from hearing the answer, yet again. The 'pay-off' here is relief from anxiety, the reassurance of knowing that the future is still predictable as well as the comforting ritual of asking a familiar question and getting a familiar reply. Another child may do exactly the same thing, but be doing it because he actually wants to pass time or chat with another person but does not have the skills needed for carrying on a 'real' conversation. Here, the pay-off is the fact that he does succeed in getting the other person talking and keeping some sort of interaction going.

Generally speaking, the motivation behind most forms of challenging behaviour seems to fall under one of five main headings, illustrated in the diagram on the next page. For the sake of illustration we have turned what your child might be thinking or feeling into words, but, of course, it will not necessarily happen like this in your child's head.

Unfortunately, it goes without saying that real life does not fit quite so neatly into boxes. Many behaviours are driven by a mix of motivations. You may find that, at different times, your child engages in a particular behaviour for different reasons or that a combination of motives is in operation at any one time. It is also especially common for the motivation for a particular behaviour to change over time. Thus, it may start as a spontaneous reaction or expression of feeling, but your child then finds out that it produces a result that is rewarding in some way. This might be the fact that an adult offers comfort or distraction or simply deals with whatever was causing distress. Your child then learns to use the same behaviour to get the same result, even when he might not actually be feeling particularly distressed.

	What might be going on in your child's head	Your child's motivation
	'Won't!' 'Go away!' 'Leave me alone!' 'I hate doing this!'	■ To avoid
	'I want ...' 'I need ...' 'Come and help me' 'More ...'	■ To communicate wants and needs
	'I just don't understand' 'I'm worried' 'I'm hurt' 'I'm angry'	■ Expressing feelings
	'That feels good' 'I made that happen!' 'Wow! Just look at that!' 'This is fun!'	■ To get stimulation
	'Somebody notice me!' 'Play with me' 'I'm lonely' 'What an interesting reaction!'	■ To get attention

Case study

Another youngster had pulled Ashley's hair quite viciously as the minibus was drawing up in front of the school one morning. This was at the end of an unusually lengthy and fraught journey to school and Ashley was extremely distressed. It took most of the morning to calm her and staff arranged for the other child to be seated well away from Ashley for at least the remaining journeys of the week. The escort made sure this happened and Ashley seemed quite happy on the way home that day. The following morning (and for the rest of the week) she displayed exactly the same distress as the minibus pulled up to school, even though nothing untoward had occurred. Efforts to distract her with pleasurable activities failed to produce the desired effect. The problem was only resolved when, in desperation, staff arranged for the minibus to stop in the staff car park and drop the children off at the side entrance to the school. A week of doing this seemed to break the pattern that had been established and Ashley then coped with the usual arrangement.

It can be difficult to make sense of the motives and purposes that lie behind the behaviour of children with autistic spectrum disorders. You may find the following points helpful when thinking about the pay-offs and purposes behind your child's behaviour.

- **Unusual sensory interests** The unusual sensory interests that were mentioned in an earlier chapter can sometimes motivate challenging behaviour. The example given in the case study below is of a child who became preoccupied with throwing objects. This is the sort of behaviour that we might normally think of as aggressive, but, for William, the motive was simply the pleasure or stimulation he seemed to get from watching the objects move across his field of vision. A fascination with certain textures occasionally leads to inappropriate touching. For the child, the motivation is purely to do with the sensory aspects of the experience, but it is easy to see how this behaviour could be seen in quite a different light.

Case study

William had started to develop some encouraging play skills, but this suddenly came to a halt when he started to throw everything he got his hands on. When his mother stood back and observed him, she realised that whenever he threw, he cocked his head on one side and seemed to be throwing objects so that they moved diagonally across his field of vision. He kept looking straight ahead, but watched the movement out of the corner of his eye. He seemed to find this visual sensation very rewarding and this knowledge helped his mother. Rather than treat this behaviour as attention seeking, which was her first hunch, she tried to find toys and activities that incorporated strong visual pay-offs. She introduced him to various types of ball-run and this seemed to help William move forward again.

Case study

In Chapter 2, we mentioned the problems presented by Mark's spitting. This pattern almost certainly became established because of the sensory pleasure it gave Mark. As well as drawing in his saliva, he liked to watch the patterns that it created as it soaked into his clothing. There were two important strands to the way staff tried to tackle this problem. As soon as Mark spat on a surface, staff would try to wipe it up (in a very low-key manner), so that the sensory pay-off was reduced. They also tried to develop Mark's interests and skills in other forms of visual reward. A lot of use was made of finger paints and cornflour and water mixtures.

- **A need for order** The need to have some part of the physical environment arranged in a very specific way can be a very strong drive. The child's attempts to impose this order on the world around him and high levels of anxiety that occur if the environment is not just so can be a significant source of problem behaviour.

Case study

John was a very powerfully built 14-year-old attending a school for children with severe learning difficulties. Although he was not expected to join the circle time that started each day, he would often become agitated at these times. Frequently this culminated in him charging across the room, trying to push one of the students in the circle to the ground and attempting to grab their chair. Staff always intervened and they assumed that John's grab for the chair was prelude to him throwing it at someone. John's real motivation only became apparent on a day when there was an empty chair in the circle. He made his usual dash, but this time grabbed the empty chair and, rather than throwing it at anyone, put it back in its 'proper' place at the table.

Though obviously very serious, his apparent attacks on others were not actually intended as such. John's focus was on restoring his idea of physical order in the classroom. Having the chairs in a circle clearly challenged his idea of how things should be. Staff responded to this difficulty by working on John's understanding of a picture timetable so that he was able to understand that the chairs would be out of place for only a limited period of time. The duration of circle time was also initially reduced, but was then gradually extended again. At the end of circle time John was given responsibility for restoring order.

- *Just* **attention seeking?** Be careful about explaining behaviour in terms of attention seeking. Overall, this is probably less common in children with autistic spectrum disorders simply because, on average, they tend to be less motivated by contact and interaction with people than other children are. Where it is the motivation behind behaviour, however, it is very important not to dismiss it as '*just* attention seeking'. Getting attention from others is a very basic need and motivation. It is actually something we would want to encourage in a child with autism, but, of course, we would also need to teach the child how to get attention in an acceptable way.

- **Making something happen** Never underestimate the need to make something happen as a motive for behaviour. This can be a response to boredom, but often children (and many adults!) seem to enjoy the sense of power and excitement that comes from 'making a splash'.

- **Rituals and habits** Some challenging behaviour seems to almost become part of a ritual or else a very strong habit. Your child may have had an experience similar to Ashley's in the example above. With some children, even a single experience like this can create a very powerful association, so that they then react in the same way when they encounter those situations again, even though the original cause of the problem is no longer present.

- **Pain and illness** Always consider the possibility that your child may be experiencing some sort of physical problem, such as earache or toothache. If your child appears to be very distressed, there does not seem to be a reaction to any external trigger and there seems to be no obvious purpose to the behaviour, then you should consider consulting your family doctor. Even where a child has some communication skills, he may not realise that he needs to inform someone before anything can be done about the problem.

Despite these difficulties, it is almost always helpful to try and get some sense of the meaning or purpose that lies behind a particular challenging behaviour. If it seems to be mainly motivated by avoidance or is an expression of distress, you need to pay particular attention to all the preventive strategies that were discussed in Chapters 3 and 4. If the problem seems to be driven by your child trying to get things or gain attention, then there is a good chance that improved communication skills will need to be part of the long-term solution. Where your child appears to be getting some sort of stimulation from the behaviour, you will probably need to help him develop other forms of play or constructive activity. In the longer term, you also need to consider what skills your child needs to learn in order to cope better with the particular situations and demands that, currently, may be causing difficulties. The rest of this chapter offers guidance about selecting skills and behaviours that, if taught or encouraged over the longer term, will help to replace current problems.

Replacing the problem – key questions

It tends to be fairly simple to come up with a list of behaviours that you want to stop – usually the only problem is the length of the list! Deciding what you want to replace the problem with, though, can be a good deal more difficult. Answering the following questions may help.

- **What is it that you want your child to be doing when he is currently engaging in the problem behaviour?**
  In your mind's eye, try to imagine the problem solved. How is your child behaving in the situations that usually trigger the difficulty? The picture you conjure up is likely to be the ideal and will probably seem hopelessly unrealistic. Now think about how things are right now in relation to this ideal. What would be the very first step towards this goal? What would he have to do in order for you to be convinced that things were on the mend?

- **What would your child need to understand, and what skills would he need to learn, in order to help him cope better in that situation?**
  Think about the demands that the situation makes on him. What would help him to cope better with them?

- **What skills does your child need in order to achieve the same results and pay-offs but in a more acceptable way?**
  Answering this question involves thinking about what your child is trying to achieve with his behaviour. Can you teach him or help him to develop better ways to gain the same results?

- **How can you interest your child in 'better' results and pay-offs?**
  Your child may not have the skills or awareness needed to find more rewarding and motivating pay-offs from his play or other activities. He may be having to make do with the results his actions and behaviour currently achieve for want of anything better.

- **What does your child currently do that is *not* a problem?**
  Take stock of your child's skills and think about what he is actually doing when he is not behaving in a challenging way. This does not mean just looking at his strengths, but, rather, considering all the behaviour that is so easy to overlook simply because it is neither especially good nor especially bad.

Case study

Shelagh's mother had repeated problems when she took her to the supermarket. There didn't seem to be any consistent triggers to the tantrums that kept erupting. Shelagh just seemed to get wound up by the whole business of going shopping and her mum was sure that her own state of tension and anticipating trouble did not help matters. Leaving Shelagh at home would have been the obvious solution, but she had no one to look after her. When she thought about what she actually wanted Shelagh to do when they were in the supermarket, she realised the answer was 'nothing' and that this was actually part of the problem. Shelagh didn't actually know how to occupy herself and fill time. In the supermarket she was bored. She found all the bustle quite stressful and she had no way to take her mind off her worries. The tantrums seemed to be partly a reaction to overload and partly a way to get the reassurance of a predictable reaction from her mother. Shelagh's teacher suggested giving her the job of pushing the trolley or getting specific items from the shelves, using picture cues. Her mother was not sure that Shelagh was ready for this yet. She decided to work on her daughter's ability to occupy herself. She realised that Shelagh was beginning to show a growing interest in music and so decided to encourage this, as well as teach her how to use a personal stereo. Soon Shelagh was willing to listen to it in the supermarket and doing this seemed to reduce her levels of anxiety. Tantrums became less frequent as a consequence. As well as taking the stereo and a supply of tapes in her backpack, her mum also included a couple of the catalogues that Shelagh seemed to enjoy leafing through. These provided a back-up form of diversion and entertainment.

Replacing the problem – key strategies

The answers to these questions should help you to identify which new skills and behaviours you need to teach and encourage. These are likely to be crucial in any longer-term solution to the problems that concern you most. When you are having to respond to, and deal with, challenging behaviour day in and day out, it is very easy to become focused on the here and now. The idea of taking a longer-term perspective can seem like an impossible and unrealistic luxury. Difficult though it can be, it is essential not to lose sight of longer-term goals, even though you may not see any immediate benefit or gain in terms of your child's behaviour. For very many children with autistic spectrum disorders, the key to resolving behaviour problems lies in the gradual development of their skills and understanding and the systematic encouragement of other ways of behaving.

When you are getting down to planning in detail, it is helpful to think in terms of the following four broad strategies.

Teaching new ways to achieve the old pay-off

Earlier in this chapter, we outlined the main motives that tend to lie behind most challenging behaviour. In Step 5 of the Eight-step Plan, you pool all the information you have – your knowledge of your child, observations of where and when the problems occur, what it seems to achieve and so on – with the aim of working out what pay-off may be driving a particular behaviour.

If you are reasonably sure that you have identified the pay-off, then the first thing to think about is whether or not you can teach or encourage alternative ways for your child to achieve the same results. This means considering two important questions.

- **Is the pay-off acceptable?** Although the behaviour that your child uses to achieve his particular goal is a problem, is the goal itself reasonable? It helps to think in terms of other children at a similar level of development who do not have an autistic spectrum disorder. Is this a goal that usually motivates them and do they usually have (or develop) the skills to achieve it?
- **Can you identify other, more appropriate ways for your child to achieve his goal?** What skills will he need to learn or use more effectively?

In the final part of this chapter, we look at some of the skills that, in our experience, make the biggest contributions to reducing your child's need to resort to challenging behaviour.

Case study

Mohinder was only six, but in danger of running up significant plumber's bills! Whenever he was in the garden at home or in the school playground, he was completely preoccupied with dropping sticks and stones down the drain – apparently deriving great pleasure from the splash. Apart from the practical problem of unblocking drains, there were concerns about possible health risks and the way that this cut Mohinder off from other forms of play. He completely ignored his older brothers as well as all the play equipment that his parents had installed in their garden. Apart from the practical problem of monitoring what he got up to, his parents were concerned that their nagging was going to damage their relationship with him. They decided to try and build on his fascination while also channelling it into a more acceptable form. In school and at home he was provided with a bucket of water, a length of plastic drainpipe and a range of floating and sinking objects. Mohinder seemed fascinated by being able to see objects emerge from the pipe and showed a brief but strong interest in this new form of play. He abandoned the drains, then mysteriously gave up this fascination altogether. He began to play on the swing and the climbing frame with his brothers. The same change also occurred at school. Staff suspected that part of the attraction of playing with the drains had been the adult attention that it generated.

Case study

Most of Ian's play was solitary and highly repetitive, but he seemed to come alive in soft play. He often 'asked' to go there by leading staff to the classroom door. They would make every effort to take him there as often as they could, but, for obvious reasons, this was not always possible. Ian did not have the language skills to understand why sometimes he could and sometimes he could not go there and, when he could not, he would react with increasingly serious tantrums. Staff decided to tackle this problem by finding a way to teach Ian how to understand when soft play was, and was not, available as an option. They took a photograph of him playing there and this was displayed on the classroom door whenever the soft play option could be provided. When Ian led staff to the door and the picture was displayed, staff drew his attention to it and took it with them to soft play. At any other time, staff would point to the space on the door where the picture would usually be displayed and say 'soft play later'. Although this initially led to the same tantrums as before, the frequency of requests and tantrums when the picture was not displayed reduced substantially over time.

Case study

Although Jamie was coping well with the academic demands of a mainstream primary school, playground problems and isolation were increasing as he moved into Key Stage 2. His old methods of involving others in play – running up to them, growling in their faces and expecting this to lead to chase games – were no longer working. By and large, other youngsters had moved on to more sophisticated forms of play. They were beginning to get fed up with Jamie's tactics and he was beginning to be distressed and angry at his increasing isolation. His teacher decided to establish a circle of friends for the specific purpose of teaching Jamie how to play a small range of playground games. She decided to use more mature Year 5 and 6 pupils for this purpose. They selected some of the games that were currently popular among Jamie's classmates and provided individualised coaching for him. His classmates were then brought into these games and into the circle. The older pupils then helped supervise playground sessions where Jamie played them with his classmates out in the playground.

Learning new skills to achieve new pay-offs

Children with autistic spectrum disorders often appear to be trapped within a very restricted world. They may not be aware of, or interested in, many of the experiences or pay-offs that motivate the behaviour of other youngsters. This applies particularly to their interest in other people – to enjoying their company and attention or wanting to please them. In fact, their reactions may be so difficult to read or they may seem so stressed, that adults and other children may gradually back off or even feel like giving up any attempts to interact. In a similar way, repetitive and highly focused patterns of play may mean that your child never has the chance to discover all the other ways of having fun with toys. He may be so hooked on the sound of a toy crashing to the floor, for example, that he never learns what else it can do. He may never be motivated or give himself the chance to develop the skills needed to operate it in a more sophisticated way.

Helping children with autistic spectrum disorders to break out of the confines of their world is a difficult, but essential goal. It is necessary to reduce levels of stress and anxiety in order to increase your child's openness to new experiences. However, it is important to then build on this by trying to show your child what else the world has to offer. Often, this will mean trying to extend your child's play – building on the existing, repetitive patterns, so that they become more complex or flexible. Frequently, the first step in this process is one of helping your child to tolerate an adult's company and attention, working towards developing his active enjoyment of play with another person.

Case study

Earlier in this chapter, we mentioned William's habit of throwing things and the fact that it was the visual sensations that seemed to be motivating the behaviour. He appeared to gain the same pay-off from a ball-run, where the ball followed a very distinct zigzag pattern. A similar piece of equipment that involved simple wooden cars rather than balls was introduced and William began to take an interest in the cars themselves. His mother also found a ball run that William had to assemble before using, by stacking the components of a tower. This helped to move him towards enjoying simple constructional play.

Case study

When Kyle first started at a specialist unit for children with autism he actively avoided all forms of contact with other people. He would hide under furniture, block his ears, screw up his eyes and scream for prolonged periods. This seemed, in part, to be an expression of his distress but increasingly it became a way of blotting out others. The intensity of Kyle's reaction gradually reduced as he became familiar with the very structured routines in the unit. The major achievement of his first year in the unit, however, was the result of the staff's attempts to show him that contact with other people could be enjoyable. Daily one-to-one sessions were run in a separate room that contained two sets of the small number of objects known to appeal to Kyle. Initially, the focus was on him simply tolerating the adult being nearby. Gradually the adult began to copy Kyle's actions and vocalisations. If these involved the objects in the room, the adult would play with 'her' set. Very gradually, Kyle showed awareness of – and took pleasure in – the fact that the adult's actions were linked to his. Eventually, with careful timing and pauses by the adult, this developed into a simple form of taking turns. Kyle began to experiment by varying his actions and then waiting for the adult to reply. Over time, a real sense of shared enjoyment began to develop and Kyle began to spontaneously initiate contact with other adults outside these sessions.

Developing skills to cope

In Chapters 3 and 4 the main emphasis was on what we could do to reduce the stress and difficulties experienced by children with autistic spectrum disorders. This involved altering the environment, changing what was expected and modifying demands. The focus was on adapting your child's world so as to take account of his difficulties. By itself, this is likely to contribute significantly to your child's ability to cope and pick up new skills. In a structured environment, with demands and expectations that he is able to understand, he will not need to devote so much time and effort to dealing with his anxiety.

As well as accommodating your child's difficulties, it is important to think in terms of actively extending or developing skills that might help him to cope better. This means looking at those situations that trigger the challenging behaviour and trying to identify what your child would need to know and do in order to handle the situation more easily. Some of the techniques mentioned in earlier chapters are not just methods of adapting the environment, but also help to develop coping skills. By using social stories, for example, you help to spell out expectations, but you also develop new skills and encourage understanding of other people's perspectives. Similarly, teaching your child to make sense of a picture timetable is not just a way of modifying and clarifying the demands you are making on him, you are also extending his independence and giving him a way of managing his own anxiety.

Case study

Andrew was finding it increasingly difficult to cope with the combination of the language and social demands of his mainstream education classroom. Whenever the teacher was involved in lengthy explanations or instructions, he would become anxious and then agitated. Often this would result in him calling out and challenging the teacher's explanation or even competence. Usually the classroom assistant dealt with this by coaxing Andrew to leave the lesson in order to calm down. A more effective, though still partial solution, was achieved by encouraging Andrew to be more aware of his own stress levels, recognize his limits and take avoiding action. Rather than continue to take responsibility for him, the assistant periodically reminded Andrew to assess his own levels of stress and record it on a line marked from 1 to 5. For those occasions when he felt too stressed, Andrew was given a card that he had to show to the teacher that allowed him to leave the classroom with no questions asked. Though his use of his 'Get out of jail card', as it became known, had to be monitored, knowing that this was available did seem to help him cope better.

At just turned five, Joe could not accept that other people had birthdays and parties when it was not his. He became very upset if he did not get presents or if he could not blow out the candles. This was a problem at school and his parents feared that he would not be invited to children's parties as a result. Although a social story had been tried, this seemed too abstract, despite using photographs of a real birthday party. His parents and teacher decided to try and develop both his understanding and the skills that would allow him to respond differently in this situation. Over the weeks before the next birthday celebrations were due to occur, his parents played 'having a birthday' using a variety of cuddly toys. One toy had the birthday and blew out the candles on the cake while the others gave presents (which Joe helped to choose and wrap) and sang 'Happy Birthday'. Joe managed to cope with the next birthday party. Though he still had some difficulty hiding his disappointment, he at least had a better idea of what he should do and could be praised for trying these alternative behaviours. It is also likely that all the rehearsal helped make him less sensitive to the situation.

Encouraging alternative behaviour

This strategy consists of deliberately trying to encourage any behaviour that is *not* the problem (which is what we mean by 'alternative behaviour') *and* is considered to be acceptable. The underlying principle is actually fairly straightforward. It consists of literally trying to replace the problem on the basis that the more time your child spends doing things that are acceptable, the less time there is for behaviour that is unacceptable.

This approach is especially useful when you have been unable to work out the motivation or pay-off that is driving your child's behaviour. It is also a very useful way of avoiding the trap that can be very easy to fall into, whether your child has any sort of difficulty or not – the temptation to leave well alone if your child is getting on quietly, only responding when a problem crops up.

In practice, this broad approach can be broken down into a number of specific tactics.

- **Encouraging behaviour that is directly incompatible with the problem behaviour**
  The trick is to identify some behaviour that is physically incompatible with the problem. This may be something that your child does spontaneously or you may need to teach and prompt a new behaviour. An example of this is a very common approach to reducing hand flapping. Rather than focusing directly on discouraging the flapping, the youngster is encouraged and rewarded for keeping his hands in his pockets. While his hands are in his pockets, he will not be physically able to flap. In Chapter 2 we mentioned Lisa who used slapping as a way of gaining attention and starting an interaction with adults. Her parents approached the problem by trying to intercept her slap and turn it into a stroke. They reasoned that slapping and stroking were mutually incompatible and there was the additional bonus that the stroking would achieve the same result for Lisa, but in a much more acceptable way for both parties.

Case study

In Chapter 2, we described the disruption that Sally caused by interfering with other people's property when she was moving around the classroom. Her teacher's first response was to reward her whenever she was sitting down. By itself, this reduced the problems simply because, to a significant degree, being in her seat was incompatible with the behaviour that triggered the conflict with her classmates.

- **Rewarding positive behaviour** It will not always be possible to think of something that is incompatible with the problem behaviour or it may be very difficult to teach or prompt it directly. The alternative is to deliberately encourage any forms of behaviour that seem to be acceptable or constructive. This means not just focusing on times when your child behaves, though it is vital to do this as well. It also means encouraging your child when he is playing constructively or cooperatively or simply occupying himself in some way. When you follow this sort of strategy systematically, you are doing three important things:
  - helping to develop and encourage skills and behaviours that are useful or enjoyable to the child and might help to 'squeeze out' the problem
  - ensuring that your child has plenty of positive experiences so he is less motivated to seek these by engaging in negative behaviour
  - showing your child how to get positive responses from you, but on your terms, not his.
- It is particularly useful and important to use this approach if you feel that your child's behaviour is motivated by the reaction he gets from you or other adults in the environment.

Case study

Gary attended a school for youngsters with severe learning difficulties. During the more formal 'work' sessions in the morning, there were often problems resulting from him grabbing hold of the leg of any member of staff who was nearby. He often grinned while doing this, but did not appear to be intending to cause physical harm. However, as he was a large 14-year-old, it felt quite intimidating and it could take several minutes to persuade him to loosen his grip. Staff members were not sure if Gary liked the fuss and attention or was using this as a way of avoiding tasks. They decided to focus on the 90 per cent of the time that Gary was not creating difficulties and make use of his particular enthusiasm for music. His teacher prepared a simple star chart—just the outlines of five stars on a piece of laminated card. Staff made a conscious effort to focus on occasions when Gary was actually getting on with his work, any instances when he responded appropriately to staff instructions, and situations where they were close to him and he did not grab. As well as lots of praise and 'high fives', staff also gave Gary a gold star, which they helped him to stick onto one of the outlines. When Gary managed to fill in all five of the outlines, he was allowed to listen to his personal stereo for five minutes.

- **'Clock watching' – giving rewards for nothing!** For all sorts of practical reasons, it can be hard to spot examples of positive behaviour and reward them consistently. It may be difficult to watch your child all the time or you may feel that there is not much positive behaviour to actually encourage. It could be that what you really want is for your child just to get on quietly, doing something on his own. One way to approach this is really a variation on the approach described in the last chapter. Rather than focusing on a particular behaviour that you want to encourage, you reward your child at regular intervals, provided the problem behaviour has not occurred. What you are doing, in effect, is encouraging anything that is not the problem. If you want to try this approach, you need to follow these steps.

- Start with a relatively short interval of time. This must be less than the gap that there usually is between instances of the problem behaviour. For example, if your child seems to be fighting with his sister every 25 or 30 minutes, aim to reward the non-occurrence of this behaviour every 15 or 20 minutes.
- To help you keep track of the time, you may want to use a ringing kitchen timer.
- As far as possible, the reward that you give should be at least as motivating as the pay-off that your child seems to be getting from his problem behaviour. Consider using your child's obsessions as motivators.

■ Your child does not need to understand the concept of time for this approach to work, but you may find that he starts to anticipate the ringing of the timer or, at least, learns to associate it with the reward. Of course, this approach, like the previous one, depends on you being able to identify a suitable reward (there are more tips on this topic in Chapter 8). Again, like the previous approach, this works best where your child's behaviour seems to be driven by adult reactions. It is also useful when you think your child's motive is to get stimulation, whether this is because he is bored or enjoys the intensity and excitement that his behaviour creates.

Case study

In Chapter 6, we described how Hannah's teachers helped reduce her preoccupation with bringing her interest in animals into every activity and conversation. As well as offering her guaranteed opportunities to talk about animals, she earned rewards for each interval of time in which she managed to avoid mentioning the subject.

Case study

When Charlie first entered his school for children with severe learning disabilities, he created havoc in his classroom with his constant running round and climbing on window ledges and radiators. Staff tackled the problem by setting up daily short one-to-one sessions in a room that contained only two chairs. Charlie was prompted to sit on one and almost immediately rewarded for 'good sitting' by being given a small piece of chocolate, which was always kept in the same container. He was then directed to sit on the other chair and was similarly rewarded. This process was practised time after time, with the adult choosing the chair at random. Gradually he was required to sit for slightly longer and a ringing timer was introduced to signal when the reward would be available. Once he had learned to remain seated for two minutes, the same procedure was used in the ordinary classroom during a particularly structured part of the morning. Although Charlie remained a very active youngster, the amount of time that he spent sitting gradually increased. Staff also reduced their reactions to the times when he did leave his seat as it became apparent that he was beginning to enjoy playing chase games.

seem to have problems in coping with more open-ended conversations. Classroom staff tackled the problem in two ways. Hannah was given a sticker for every 20 minutes that she did not mention any kind of animal (with her classmates enthusiastically monitoring this). She was also offered a short daily session with the classroom support assistant, when she could talk and write about animals. In addition, the school also embarked on the much more difficult and longer-term project of enhancing Hannah's conversational skills.

- **Timetabling obsessions and rituals** It is important that your child knows, or quickly learns, that you are not trying to take away the favourite activity for good. Particularly in the early stages, try to build access to the activity into your child's routine. If possible, try to show this on a picture timetable – it provides reassurance and may be a useful incentive.

Case study

Ross has complex difficulties and attends an SLD school. When he was 12, he developed a very strong interest in touching other people's skin. This seemed to be part of a wider interest in soft textures, but he also seemed to quite like the startled or disapproving reaction that this behaviour triggered. Ross was given a special 'feely' bag, filled with nice textures, which were changed regularly. When he went to touch others, he was told 'no' and was redirected to the bag. He was also provided with a short, one-to-one session each day, when he played rough and tumble-type games with a familiar adult. Any touching was redirected into a game, so that he had a way of initiating interaction without inappropriate touching.

Case study

Clare was 10 and forever taking herself off to the toilet. This was usually to go through a little ritual of running a little water into each of the washbasins, rather than because she needed the toilet. This did not seem to be driven by any strong anxiety, so her teacher decided to gradually wean her off the habit, while watching closely for any adverse reaction. She provided Clare with ten tickets and she was required to hand one in each time she went to the toilet. The total that she started with each day was then gradually reduced. It was felt that three visits during lesson time would be a reasonable target and would allow her a little bit of 'down time'.

Fears and phobias

It is not uncommon for children with autistic spectrum disorders to develop extreme fears or phobias. Sometimes only a single frightening encounter or unpleasant experience is enough. To us, the child's reaction may appear to be quite out of proportion to the original experience or the risk of its repetition. Alternatively, the source of the fear may seem quite incomprehensible to an adult. The child may be tuning in to something in the environment that we may not be aware of or it may be something that we would never think of as frightening. The fear may then trigger a tantrum or an attempt to avoid the source of the fear, which can then be very difficult to deal with (and very distressing for all concerned). Unfortunately, the more successful the child is at avoiding the situation, the stronger the fear may become and the more motivated the child will be to continue avoiding it.

What new skills might help?

The main focus of this chapter has been the need to help your child learn new skills which will contribute to improved behaviour. We have especially emphasised the development of new ways for your child to get the pay-offs that motivate him and skills that help him cope with difficult situations. Here we simply list a selection of skills and behaviours that, in our experience, can play an important part in reducing the likelihood of challenging behaviour. None of these offer quick fixes – indeed, many of the skills will need careful teaching and encouragement sustained over quite long periods of time. When you are working on these skills, however, you are actually dealing directly with the core of your child's difficulties. If you are able to make headway, then you are not just helping to reduce the likelihood that your child will need to resort to challenging behaviour, you are also making a broader, longer-term, contribution to your child's well-being and competence.

For ease of reference, we have grouped the skills into sections corresponding to the triad of impairments. Before you read further, though, we should stress that this list is highly selective and not intended as a description or syllabus of all the skills that a child with an autistic spectrum disorder might need to learn. It is here to act as a reminder of the skills and behaviours that you might need to consider teaching so as to provide your child with alternatives to his current problem behaviour. It is beyond the scope of this book to go into the details of how to teach these skills, but, in the Further Reading section, we suggest some useful publications that do provide such guidance.

Developing communication skills

From the earlier part of this chapter where we considered the meaning of challenging behaviour, it will be obvious that difficulties with communication can often be the root cause. Your child may not have any alternative way to express what he wants or does not want. He may be reacting to the frustration of not being able to get his message across or of not understanding what people are trying to tell him. Your child may simply fail to understand what he is being expected or told to do and may not even be aware that his behaviour is creating a problem. Think about the communication skills that your child does possess and if it may be worth considering working on any of the following.

- **Pointing** This is one of the most powerful and versatile forms of communication. Teaching pointing not only helps your child to express his needs, but also helps him to realise that communicating with others is useful and fun. It helps lay essential foundations for other forms of communication.
- **Understanding pictures** Understanding the relationship between a picture or some form of symbol and what it represents provides a way in to a whole range of communication strategies.
- **Alternative ways of communicating – using pictures and symbols** This can help your child to communicate about things outside the here and now. It makes the most of your child's visual strengths and reduces the demand on certain skills that can be particular problems for children with autistic spectrum disorders. These alternative forms of communication do help some children to develop spoken language. Just as importantly, there is *no* evidence that using pictures, symbols or signs holds back speech. Currently, the Picture Exchange Communication System is increasingly being used with children with autism.

- **Gaining attention** Many children with autism do not realise that they have to gain someone's attention before starting to communicate, whatever method of communication they use.

- **Sharing a focus of attention** This involves the child paying attention to the same thing as the adult *and* being aware that the adult is also sharing the same focus of attention (often shown by the child's gaze alternating between the object and the adult's face). This is an essential skill for building up understanding of language and is a basic building block in the development of the child's ability to interact with other people.

- **Learning to listen** Many children will need to be taught and encouraged to pay attention to their own name and speech in general. Many children do not seem to instinctively recognize that human speech is a special sort of sound. They seem to treat it as no more significant than other noises in the environment.

- **Asking for help** If a child understands that adults are able and willing to help, and if he has some way to request help, this reduces the likelihood that frustration or anxiety will lead to a full-blown tantrum or panic attack.

- **Understanding 'first ..., then ...'** Understanding this concept, by means of pictures or words, is a vital first step in helping your child to anticipate what is about to happen. It is also the beginning of you and your child learning to negotiate with each other.

- **Understanding a picture timetable** This extends your child's ability to anticipate and make sense of the overall routine and structure of his day. It can also help to extend your child's ability to act independently and manage his own anxiety.

- **Coping with non-literal language** As it is almost impossible for adults to totally avoid non-literal language, it can be helpful to directly teach your child the meaning of the commonest 'turns of speech'.

- **Self-monitoring** Particularly with older and more verbal children, it is important to develop their ability to recognize when something doesn't make sense. They also need to know how to ask for repetition or additional explanation.

- **Labelling feelings** If a child is helped to identify and label at least a small range of basic feelings in himself, he can then be encouraged to tell you, rather than simply react to, particular triggers that might make him angry or frightened. This can also contribute to his recognition and understanding of other people's feelings – an important social skill.

Developing social interaction and understanding

A lack of interest in contact with other people means that children with an autistic spectrum disorder are cut off from a crucial source of motivation, information and enjoyment. Even with children who are interested in contact with others, significant problems may result from them not understanding the unwritten rules about how to behave in particular situations. Problems in interpreting the intentions and reactions of others can also lead to substantial difficulties. With more able children, this may create a real barrier to establishing close friendships. In turn, it can contribute to feelings of anger, isolation or anxiety that may trigger a range of challenging behaviours.

Helping your child to develop certain sorts of social skills and understanding can reduce the likelihood of challenging behaviour occurring.

- **Learning to enjoy people** You may need to start with the more basic aim of helping your child just to tolerate being close to, or touching, another person. If you can then build up your child's enjoyment of and interest in contact with you, you are introducing him to a fundamental source of motivation – attention from another person. This may motivate him to communicate and give you an important means of rewarding and influencing his behaviour (using praise and attention).

■ **Building interactive games** With very young children, or those at a very early developmental level, it can be exceptionally helpful to build up simple interactive play routines. As well as developing your child's interest and enjoyment in people, this develops skills and understanding that are critical for communication.

■ **Learning the rules of the game** Much of Chapter 3 was about the importance of spelling out the unwritten rules governing specific situations and finding a way of putting these in a form that your child can understand and recall.

■ **Friendship skills** The understanding and skills used in building and maintaining friendships are tremendously complex. Though it is not yet possible to analyse and teach all the many skills that are involved, certain critical skills have been identified. These include giving compliments, dealing with criticism, accepting suggestions, sharing and reciprocating (in conversation and in the directing of activities), listening to other people and being aware of their reactions. Methods for helping children to learn these skills, and put them into practice in live situations, are still at an early stage. Close monitoring and tutoring by an adult, coaching and modelling by peers, combined with rehearsal and role play, are all likely to be essential ingredients.

■ **Understanding other people** Again, methods of helping people with autistic spectrum disorders to better understand other people's beliefs, feelings and intentions are still at a relatively early stage. Some guidance is now available and studies show that improvements can be maintained over quite long periods. Work continues into finding ways to help children use these skills flexibly in new situations.

■ **Developing self-control** Although this is also a very complex and demanding skill, it is possible to help youngsters towards this goal. Being aware of, and able to identify, their own feelings is an important first step. Some children may be able to recognise the danger signals that tell them they are about to lose self-control. Assisting them to recognise their own limits and teaching them strategies for getting out of the situation or seeking help can be very useful. Some youngsters are also able to learn routines for calming themselves.

Responding to problems of inflexible thinking and behaviour

With challenging behaviour that is linked to problems of inflexibility, it is especially useful to think in terms of developing new skills. Some of these problems seem to be reactions to, or ways of coping with, anxiety. Sometimes such patterns of behaviour may reflect the fact that your child lacks the skills to play, interact or communicate in any other way. Skills that may need to be taught include the following.

■ **Anticipating future events** Anything that allows your child to anticipate and make sense of what is going to happen is likely to lower anxiety levels. This, in turn, may reduce his need to impose routines and rituals or get involved in repetitive behaviour.

■ **Tolerating change and uncertainty** The ability to cope with change and uncertainty needs to be treated as a learned skill. It is sometimes possible to teach youngsters alternative ways of dealing with their anxiety – as when someone who repetitively asks questions about forthcoming events is encouraged to use a timetable to provide the necessary reassurance.

- **Building on obsessions** One of the commonest ways of dealing with highly repetitive or obsessional activities is to attempt to extend them into more complex and appropriate forms of play. It may be possible to introduce a social dimension to the activity. Sometimes the focus is on gradually building variations into the activity – different materials, a wider range of actions and so on.
- **Developing play skills** Building on obsessions in the way just outlined is one example of the broader strategy of extending your child's play. The intention is to develop your child's interests and skills so that he learns how to get different and, hopefully, more motivating pay-offs from his activities.

The teaching and encouragement of new skills and behaviours is an absolutely central strategy – not only when trying to tackle specific problem behaviours, but also in helping to prevent problems from emerging in the first place. It is impossible to separate the long-term process of education from the day-to-day job of managing behaviour. The differing demands and expectations of school and home may produce varying reactions, requiring different strategies in the two settings. However, when it comes to the task of choosing the new skills and behaviours that need to be targeted, and finding ways of developing them, parents and school staff will need to work in close collaboration.

8
Motivating change – making sure that new behaviour achieves positive results

Introduction

In the previous chapter, we explained the importance of teaching new skills and encouraging alternative forms of behaviour in any long-term plan for dealing with challenging behaviour. We suggested thinking in terms of three broad categories:

- skills that would help your child cope better with specific situations
- new skills and behaviours that provide your child with better ways of getting the pay-offs that currently motivate his behaviour or offer him the opportunity to experience new rewards and consequences
- any sort of acceptable behaviour, especially if it is incompatible with the current problem.

A detailed description of all the techniques that you might use to teach these new skills is beyond the scope of this book. However, in any effort to teach a new skill or encourage a new way of behaving, you are almost certain to encounter the same problem: how do you motivate your child to change? If you think about the last time you attempted to change one of your own patterns of behaviour or learn a new skill, you may find that this is not just a problem experienced by people with an autistic spectrum disorder! From your child's point of view, you are actually asking him to do two things, both of which might provoke him to ask, 'Why should I?' You are asking him to give up a tried and tested way of behaving that might be working perfectly well (from his point of view) *and* you are expecting him to go to the trouble of learning something new. The aim of this chapter is to answer the question: how do we ensure that these new skills and behaviours achieve positive results for your child, so that he is motivated to learn and change?

A note about terminology

In this chapter, the words 'reward' and 'pay-off' are used interchangeably. We use them to refer to anything that follows a behaviour and increases the chances of your child behaving in that way in the future. It is important to bear in mind two rather different sorts of reward or pay-off:

- those that might be described as 'natural consequences' – the direct effects of the skill or the behaviour, such as the sensory stimulation or excitement he gets when he throws a toy or the fact that using his communication board means that he is able to communicate his needs

- those that are deliberately provided in order to strengthen your child's motivation, such as a hug, merit award, smiley face sticker, favourite twiddler and so on.

Planning the use of rewards

Before we discuss practical techniques in more detail, we need to think about some of the basic requirements for any approach to rewarding and motivating new behaviour or skills. Whatever the nature of your child's difficulties, the strategy used has got to be able to do the following.

- **The pay-offs for new behaviour must be as good as those earned by the old behaviour** In the long run, the new behaviours and skills that you are trying to encourage must earn your child at least the same level of reward as his old ways of behaving. He must be able to achieve the same results or get rewards and pay-offs that are just as motivating (or even more so), with no more effort. One of the biggest traps is trying to prevent your child from getting the old pay-offs with his old ways of behaving, but not providing him with new ways of getting rewards.

Case study

Wayne would drink washing-up liquid whenever he got a chance and there were serious worries about the effect of this on his health. Putting it in a locked cupboard simply created other problems: he was so desperate to get at it, that there were major battles and tantrums. Although it almost seemed to be an obsession, there was definitely something about the strength of the taste or the sensation of it in his mouth that appealed to him. His mother dealt with the problem by gradually building up his interest in using the washing-up liquid in other ways. Whenever he tried to get at it, she would run a bowl of water and prompt him to put the washing-up liquid in the water rather than his mouth. She and Wayne would then spend five or ten minutes playing with the bubbles using a variety of bath toys. At first, this was just a form of distraction but, over time, he became more and more interested in the games that he and his mother played. He still got through huge quantities of washing-up liquid but his attempts to drink it gradually faded.

- **Cope with the reward gap** In the longer term, it is hoped that your child will use a skill or behave in a certain way because of the natural consequences of doing so – that is, the pay-offs that the behaviour naturally leads to. However, the early stages of learning and using any skill involve much more effort than is needed later on. In the early days, it is also likely that the new behaviour or skill will not produce the desired results – or certainly not as easily or efficiently as it will once it has been well practised. At least in the short term, therefore, we may need to provide extra, 'artificial' rewards. In the longer term, the aim and hope is that your child will begin to experience and be motivated by the natural consequences of the new skill or behaviour. However, it is important to note that some children may go on needing the extra incentive provided by the artificial rewards.

Harry was totally addicted to the TV and his computer. One or other of them had to be on all the time and there were major tantrums if they were switched off before bedtime. His father tried to set limits on these pastimes by gradually switching them off earlier and earlier. If Harry accepted this without too much trouble, he was given a 50p piece, which he saved in a jar to put towards the cost of his next computer game. This artificial reward worked, but it was an expensive solution that still fed one of his obsessions. Once Harry was not spending the whole of his evenings in front of a screen, his parents began to involve him in other activities and games, which he eventually learned to enjoy. Instead of needing a financial incentive to stop watching TV, Harry began to select the programmes he really wanted to watch (with a limit of two hours per night) and was happy to plan other activities to fill the spaces between programmes. An evening timetable was used to show the slots when he was able to choose the TV or the computer.

- **Help the child to see the connection** No matter how generous and motivating the rewards, they will not have much effect if your child cannot understand the connection. He has to be able to make and keep in mind the link between behaving in a certain way and getting a particular pay-off. Many children with autistic spectrum disorders find it especially difficult to single out and focus on the relevant features of a situation. They may not appreciate the connection, unless we can find a way to highlight it for them.
- **Take account of your child's autism** There are many ways in which people with autistic spectrum disorders seem to perceive and experience the world in a different way from the rest of us. As we mentioned in the previous point, this affects their understanding of the link between their own behaviour and its consequences. It also has a major impact on what they find motivating, something that is discussed in more detail in the next section.
- **Take account of the individual** Your knowledge of your child – his personality, strengths, likes and dislikes, as well as his autism – is vital to identifying the most effective way to motivate new behaviour.

In Chapter 7, we mentioned something called the Picture Exchange Communication System (PECS), which is now in fairly common use with children with autistic spectrum disorders who have very limited communication skills. The introduction of PECS with Pradeep illustrates how all the principles outlined above can be put into action. His main interests in life were chocolate buttons, a rubber octopus, which he flicked, and bubbles. The first step was to take good clear photos of each of these objects and mount them on card. Pradeep was then sat opposite an adult with a single card in front of him. The corresponding object was clearly in view, next to the adult. Pradeep was prompted to hand the card to the adult and then he would immediately receive a short turn with the toy (or a small piece of chocolate). Following the sequence used in PECS, he was gradually expected to do more. The prompting to hand over the picture was reduced, he had to get the picture from a communication board, which was moved further and further away, and the adult sat at a greater and greater distance from him. In the end, he was collecting the picture, going over to the adult, attracting her attention, then handing over the picture. This was always followed by immediate access to the reward.

Case study

Nicky seemed more likely to kick and pinch his mum when she was paying attention to his younger sister. It was not clear if it was his mother's attention that he wanted or simply that he enjoyed the physical contact and excitement created by his mum's attempts to persuade him to stop. He had very limited communication skills. Though these were being worked on at school, it was clearly going to be a long, long time before he would be able to ask for attention in an acceptable way. The eventual solution had two parts to it. First, his mother reduced her reaction to the unwanted behaviour to the absolute minimum – usually she would go out of the room. Second, she made a deliberate effort to give Nicky attention at very frequent intervals. This involved giving him a fairly energetic tickle or hug whenever he seemed to be paying attention to her or when he approached her. She also made sure she did this every now and then even if he was just getting on with something on his own. This appeared to provide him with a pay-off that was equivalent to the attention he was getting from the fights with his mother. On its own, ignoring him would probably not have worked as Nicky clearly had a strong need for some form of contact and interaction. It is likely that he would have found some other, probably unacceptable way to get this. By using rewards, his mum was giving him a very clear message about what were acceptable ways to get her attention. By paying him attention when he was occupying himself, she was also keeping him topped up with the sort of contact he liked and needed.

But does he really *deserve* it? Thinking about our attitudes to reward

As we discussed at the end of Chapter 2, challenging behaviour can produce some very strong reactions. When you have had to deal with the problem day in and day out, it can be very difficult to think in terms of giving rewards. Even when your child has actually done as you wanted, all the occasions when this did not happen may cast a shadow over his (and your) success. You may feel that you are entitled to expect good behaviour – that somehow this is the natural order of things. It is easy to feel grudging about giving a reward. Also, if things have got really bad, it can be much easier to think in terms of the punishments that might be deserved rather than rewards that have been earned.

Even if we are ready and willing to use rewards, there is a good chance that we will encounter other adults – in our family, the supermarket or the staffroom – who take a rather different view! It may be useful to remind yourself (and possibly some of these other people) why it is important to make use of incentives and rewards when you are trying to help your child change his behaviour.

■ It is always useful to remember how much of your own behaviour depends on rewards. Many of the things that you freely choose to do are often done for the pleasure and satisfaction you get from the activities or from the sense of self-esteem or competence that you experience. Many of your actions are influenced by the approval you gain from other people and, of course, there are the things you do for money.

- Although we are not always aware of it, many of these same rewards also influence the behaviour of children who do not present with challenging behaviour. It is nice to think that they are behaving acceptably because it is somehow in their nature to be good, but 'good' behaviour actually brings a range of very powerful pay-offs for most children.

- Sadly, despite our best efforts, the lives of many children with autistic spectrum disorders may actually be quite deprived of rewarding or motivating experiences. Many of the things that motivate and influence other children – like approval from adults or friends – may be of limited interest. Children with autistic spectrum disorders may find it especially difficult to learn many of the skills needed to gain positive experiences and reactions from their environment.

- It is far harder for any child to change a pattern of challenging behaviour than it is for a child who already behaves well to continue doing so. Giving up old habits and the rewards they bring, as well as learning new ways of behaving, all require significant effort. It is essential to recognise and find ways to motivate and reward this effort.

Finding rewards that work

Once you have decided on the new skills and behaviour that you want your child to develop, the next step is to plan ways of motivating him. This may be a lot easier said than done. Some children with autistic spectrum disorders seem remarkably self-contained. It can be extremely difficult to identify experiences that motivate or interest them. The following tips may help you.

- **Remember that a reward is what rewards!** If it does not motivate your child, then it is not a reward. If, for instance, your child does not respond to praise from a grown-up or merit stickers in his exercise book, then they are simply not rewards for him even if they do work for other children.

- **Experiment and observe** Nothing can replace your own detailed knowledge of your child. Watch what he does when he is free to choose. Experiment with novel toys and activities – one youngster's first purposeful word was motivated by his intense interest in a pair of plastic, wind-up, chattering teeth. Anything that a child freely chooses to do has potential as an incentive. By a process of trial and error and observation, try to build up a list of rewards that your child responds to.

- **Use the old results to motivate the new behaviour or skill** As we explained in the last chapter, one of the main strategies for dealing with challenging behaviour is to replace it – teaching the child a better way to achieve the same results. This applies particularly where the purpose of the behaviour is to express a need or want or get some form of stimulation. We described the way in which Nadia had learned to run out of the room so that adults would chase her, and how her environment was restructured to reduce this problem. In the longer term, Nadia's communication skills will also need to be worked on. One of the very earliest messages that we might want to target would be 'play chase with me.'

Case study

Brian became quite obsessed with throwing things. He seemed to enjoy the sensory pay-off, particularly that of the sight and sound of objects hitting the ground. In the longer term, classroom staff wanted to develop other play skills. In the short term, though, they decided to channel it into a more acceptable form, while also restricting the amount of time he spent engrossed in doing this. They taught Brian to play a form of skittles using a large sponge ball and empty drinks cans in which bells, marbles, dried peas and so on had been sealed. This allowed Brian to achieve quite a spectacular pay-off that was of just the kind that appealed to him so much, but in a more appropriate way. Regular skittles sessions were built in to his timetable, and throwing at other times was very firmly discouraged.

- **Consider using your child's special interest as a reward** Whether or not you can do this will depend on just what the interest is. You may be able to give your child a quick turn with some special object or activity as an immediate reward. It may be difficult to do this with some special interests as they may take too long to set up or require too much of your child's time. However, it may still be possible to use these as motivators in less frequent, but longer sessions. Later on in this chapter, we describe ways in which you can help your child understand this idea of 'working towards' a reward. Before using your child's special interest as a reward, think about his likely reaction when he has to stop the activity. Some children have interests that are so all-consuming that it can be very difficult to interrupt them once they have got started. Using these as incentives, therefore, may be inviting difficulties.

Case study

Suki's great passion in life was collecting toys on her visits to MacDonalds. Left to her own devices, she would play with each one in turn, in the same order that she had acquired them. Her reward for completing tasks at home or at school was to have a session with these toys and this worked very successfully. However, as her collection grew, these sessions began to take up too much time and it was decided to gradually limit the number she was allowed. She selected these at the start of the morning or afternoon and still played with them in the set order.

- **Do not overlook tangible rewards** Particularly with younger children, it is always useful to experiment with a raisin, a small fragment of chocolate or a quick bit of rough and tumble play. Our experience has also shown us that some secondary age youngsters in mainstream schools will make significant efforts to earn a very modest chocolate bar at the end of the school day!
- **You may need to 'teach' new rewards** This may sound something of a contradiction in terms. Some activities or experiences may not be rewarding to begin with, simply because your child has been reluctant to try something unfamiliar or has difficulty making sense of it. He may also lack the skills needed to join in or play, so may never have seen the point of the activity or got far enough to experience the pay-off. It is always important to keep on trying to extend the range of activities that interest and motivate your child. This means slowly familiarising him with a new game, toy or way of playing and gradually building up the skills he needs. The description of Wayne and his washing-up liquid given earlier in this chapter provides an example of this tactic.
- **Variety's the spice ...** It is always helpful to have a range of rewards to offer. For those children who are especially difficult to motivate, this may only be a distant goal. However, even if you have found a particular reward that really seems to work, it is still worth trying to extend the range of rewards that he responds to so that he does not get bored with what is on offer.

When Ravinder first started at specialist nursery, if she was left to her own devices, she would cruise around holding pairs of objects in her hand. Sometimes these had to be physically identical, sometimes it seemed to be the colour that was the important feature, but it was always two, and Ravinder seemed to get intense pleasure from looking at them. Her constant physical restlessness was creating practical management problems at home and in the nursery. It also meant that she was missing opportunities to learn new ways to play. It was decided to focus on extending her ability to remain sitting down for short periods. She was provided with a box of toys and objects specially selected to allow them to be paired up and combined in all sorts of ways. Ravinder was allowed to play with the contents only as long as she was sitting down. As soon as she started to roam, all the items were removed (including the two in her hand). Although this provoked a protest, over time Ravinder learned to sit for longer and longer. The strategy also gave adults a chance to join Ravinder in her play and so gradually extend her range of skills and interests.

By the time Joseph was ten, his habit of stroking other people's clothing had become a serious problem – particularly as he was especially keen on the texture of women's tights! Joseph did not pay any attention to the reaction of the people he touched. The behaviour did not seem to be a way of communicating or of starting off social interaction. The main pay-off appeared to be the physical sensations and pleasure that the different materials gave Joseph. To deal with this problem, he was provided with a bag that contained pieces of the materials that he most enjoyed touching. Whenever he went to touch other adults or children, he was told 'no' and redirected to the bag. He was also provided with the bag at 'choosing times' and had the opportunity to select new items to go in it.

Although she was only seven, Louisa was in danger of trashing her home as she was constantly climbing on furniture and bouncing on the sofa and chairs. She seemed to be doing this for the sheer physical pleasure that these activities gave her, and her father had very mixed feelings about trying to remove one of the few activities that she really enjoyed. The family decided to invest in a climbing frame and a trampette, which they installed in the garden. To begin with, Louisa was absolutely terrified of these strange objects. Her parents gradually coaxed her closer and closer, for longer and longer periods, by staging picnics in the garden. Once Louisa could tolerate being next to the equipment, it only required a demonstration by her older sister for her to get the hang of the new activities. This meant she now had a new and acceptable way of getting the same pay-offs. Her parents felt able to put a stop to her behaviour in the house by redirecting Louisa to the garden as soon as she started to climb or bounce. Gradually she also learned to tolerate limits on the times she could spend out there. Her parents used a picture of the equipment with a thick red line through it, which was displayed on the French windows whenever the garden was out of bounds.

Case study

Kieran's obsession with computer games was used in two ways to tackle his total lack of interest in schoolwork, which was leading him into conflict with his support assistant, then disturbing everyone else's concentration. A computer game format was used to structure his assignments for each day. He had a certain number of 'levels' to complete each day, could earn and lose 'lives' (for specific sorts of behaviour) and could earn 'golden keys' for achieving a certain standard in his work. Each key could then be exchanged at home for a fixed number of minutes on his current favourite.

Giving rewards and getting the best out of them

Systematically using rewards to motivate new skills and behaviour is different from giving your child treats. You need to plan carefully if they are going to have the impact that you want. Always remember that you are actually trying to do two things. You want your child to unlearn an old pattern, to give up whatever rewards or pay-offs were keeping that behaviour going. At the same time, you are expecting your child to take a step into the unknown, to make the effort to learn a new skill in return for a reward that may be new or uncertain. You need to make sure that you achieve the greatest impact from any rewards that you have managed to identify. These guidelines will help.

- **Plan the environment** The reward that you have chosen is not likely to have much effect if your child can simply help himself to it! You need to be especially conscious of this when you are trying to encourage communication. Make sure that these things are out of reach and think about whether or not they need to be out of sight, too. Some children may be distracted or frustrated if they can see but not get at, something they find highly motivating. It is equally important for you to plan ahead so that the rewards you are going to use are easily and immediately available.
- **Immediate and consistent – the golden rules of rewards** Especially in the early stages of learning or encouraging a new skill or behaviour, each tiny step will need maximum encouragement. This means:
  - giving the reward immediately after the action or behaviour occurs
  - giving the reward each and every time.
- **Help your child to understand the connection** Your child needs to be helped to understand the link between the new way of behaving and the rewards and pay-offs that it brings. Rewarding him immediately and consistently is one way of helping to get the message across. It is also important to explain just what he has done to earn the reward. Though it has a rather unnatural feel to it, a phrase such as 'Good sitting!' gives your child much more useful information, than simply telling him he has been a 'good boy'.
- **Reward first steps** Whether it is a new skill or a different way of reacting to a particular situation, your child will not get it right first time. None of us do when we are learning something new. You may have to break the new skill into small steps. To begin with, provide the reward for these first steps rather than a perfect performance. Your expectations and the standards you set can then be raised gradually as your child's skills develop.

- **Be generous with rewards** You have to make sure that behaving in the new way is more attractive than carrying on with old patterns, otherwise your child will not see the point. This means making sure that new behaviours and skills earn him a generous pay-off. You may find this quite a difficult personal challenge. It is very easy to feel anything but generous towards your child, especially early on, before his behaviour has really changed a great deal.

- **Use plenty of praise** Whatever reward or pay-off you start off with, always use lots of praise as well. Provided that your child does not find attention difficult to deal with, try to show your pleasure and enthusiasm. Even if your child appears to be indifferent to start with, it is still important to work towards the long-term goal of him being motivated by attention and praise from other people.

- **Help your child to anticipate rewards** Having the reward in view may create problems – your child may becoming frustrated or distracted. It can still be very helpful to remind your child of the reward that is in store, though, especially if you are unable provide it there and then. Some of the strategies that we have already mentioned in earlier chapters will help.
  - Use the 'first ..., then ...' prompt. This helps your child to understand that 'not just now' or 'wait' does not actually mean 'never, ever'.
  - Visual systems can be used to help get this message across – even at the simplest level of having a photograph or symbol that represents the reward to come.
  - Use tokens to bridge the gap. The next section outlines one approach to teaching your child to wait for the reward.

- **A part-time system** Giving this amount of attention and maintaining this level of consistency can be extremely demanding (and, in some circumstances, all but impossible). You may still be able to make headway by operating your reward system on a part-time basis.
  - Choose a part of the day when you may be able to provide the levels of attention that are required. It is helpful to pick a natural block of time, such as before playtime, after tea, up until lunch. Because these are natural breaks, they will help your child identify when the system is in operation.
  - You can also get this message across by using visual cues that show the system is in operation. Keep any rewards and equipment you are using in a distinctive container. When these are on view, they act as a reminder about the behaviour that is expected and the rewards that are available for it. Symbols or pictures can be displayed to get the same message across.

- **Thin out the rewards** Once the new pattern of behaviour or new skill is well on its way to being established, you need to gradually reduce the level of extra rewards that you have been providing. Doing this will actually strengthen your child's motivation in the longer term. This also helps to wean your child on to the natural consequences of the new skill or behaviour.
  - Gradually shift to rewarding only every other instance of the behaviour, then, perhaps, every third or fourth instance.
  - Eventually aim to vary the frequency of the reward, so that the pattern is less and less regular.

How far you can go in thinning out the reward will depend in part on your child and also on how powerful the natural pay-offs are that the behaviour provides. Many children with autistic spectrum disorders continue to need additional incentives for a long time.

Case study	Rikesh's parents felt that it was important for him to attend temple with the rest of the family, but he found it hard to remain quiet for the whole of the service. At school, Rikesh had been taught to connect a cartoon of someone making a 'ssshhhh' gesture with being quiet. As soon as he began to make a noise in temple, he was shown a picture of his father making the same gesture. The moment he quietened down, he was then allowed to have a minute or two playing with a box of his favourite twiddlers. On its own, this would have just taught him to make more noise, not less, but his parents then required him to remain quiet for longer and longer intervals before he could have the box. If he had been quiet for a while without the picture prompt, they also rewarded him with a quick twiddle.

Case study	Jonathan was in his fourth year in a mainstream school and showed very little interest in any schoolwork that was not related to his special interests. His teacher and support assistant decided to break the morning's work down into very specific, short assignments – initially, each was planned to take 10 to 15 minutes. These were listed for him at the start of the day and, in between each one, he was allowed five minutes on his dinosaur topic, provided he had completed the assignment. Gradually it proved possible to increase the length of the individual assignments, then to reduce the frequency of these rewards until he had a single 15-minute session at the end of the morning.

Bridging the gap – learning to wait for rewards

'Immediate and consistent' may be the golden rule of rewards, but there is a whole range of reasons for this not always being either practical or desirable.

- You may be in a situation where the preferred reward is simply not physically available – you cannot offer your child five minutes on his computer game when you are out shopping, for example.
- Even if the reward is to hand, it may not be practical to provide it immediately. It may cause too much of a disruption, break the child's concentration or be too difficult to get him away from the reward and back to what he was originally doing.
- The rewards that motivate your child (and this is often more of problem when your child gets older) may cost too much or require too much time to be provided very frequently.
- In the school situation, you may worry about how other children will react or the reward may be something provided at home by your child's parents.

This is where tokens may come in handy. The word 'token' is a piece of jargon that it is actually quite difficult to find an everyday replacement for. It means something tangible that is not in itself rewarding. It has to be something that you can quickly and easily give your child, immediately after he has behaved in the way that you are trying to encourage. The token is not the reward itself, but, at a later point, it is exchanged for something that is a reward. The most common example we are all familiar with is money. Some children do understand and respond to money, but it is more common to use things such as stickers, smiley face stamps or some form of plastic counter.

This sort of approach would be unlikely to work with very young children or those at a very early developmental level. Very roughly speaking, it probably requires a three- to four-year-old's level of understanding as an absolute minimum. If you feel this might be a helpful approach to use with your child, work your way through the steps that follow.

- **Choose the reward** All the points that we have made in earlier sections still apply, only more so. If your child is going to be expected to wait for the reward, then it has to be worth waiting for!

- **Choose the tokens** You can use ticks on a chart or colour in sections of a picture, but often children like something that seems a bit more extravagant, such as stickers, stars, stamps and so on. Some children may even find these rewarding in themselves. Others respond better if you use objects – plastic cubes or counters, marbles or pegs in a pegboard, for example. It may be useful to build a direct link with the reward. For instance, you could cut up a picture of the rewarding activity and give your child a section each time. When he completes the picture, he gets the reward for engaging in the behaviour that you are trying to encourage.

- **Set the price** What does your child have to do (or not do) before he gets a token? How many tokens does he have to earn, over what period of time before he gets the actual reward? There are no hard and fast rules for answering these questions but, to begin with, it is always a good idea to err on the side of generosity. You want your child to understand the system and get hooked on the reward. Keep the demands low and give lots of opportunities for success. Choose a task or a standard of behaviour that will be within your child's grasp. To begin with, provide the reward every time your child manages to get five or so of the tokens.

- **Storing and displaying the tokens** You need a system for storing and displaying the tokens as they are earned. Your child does not need to be able to count, he just needs to be able to see easily how many tokens he has earned and how far there is to go before he will be given the reward. The very simplest system would be a chart with a strip divided into, say, four squares. Each of the squares would be big enough to hold a single sticker or stamp. When your child has filled each of the squares, he gets the reward. It can be helpful to include a picture or symbol at the end of the line illustrating the reward.

- **Teaching what the tokens are worth** Tokens mean nothing in themselves. Your child will only start to be motivated by them once he understands what they can be swopped for and how the system works. The key to this is to set up the situation so that your child has lots of opportunities to make two essential links. First, between his behaviour and getting the token and, second, between the token and the back-up reward. To build up this understanding, you need to ensure the following.
  - Create lots of opportunities for your child to earn tokens and reward him with them consistently and immediately. At this stage, you also need to set up the situation so that the back-up reward is readily available.
  - If you are using the sort of chart outlined in the last point, start off by leaving just the last space blank. As soon as he earns a sticker, prompt him to (or let him watch you) fill in the final space, then immediately get him to give you the completed chart so that you can exchange it for the chosen reward.
  - Once he understands that he can swop the completed chart for the reward, introduce the idea that the tokens have to be collected over a period of time. Leave two blanks on the chart, but try to set things up so that there is only a small delay between him earning the final two tokens and then swapping it for the back-up reward. Continue with this process until he is used to starting with a blank chart.

■ **Raise demands gradually** Once your child seems to understand how the system works, you can think about gradually raising demands. You can approach this in a number of ways:

● expect a bit more for each token. For instance, a slightly longer period of time without a particular problem

● increase the number of tokens he has to get before he is given the reward

● introduce a delay between collecting the tokens and exchanging them for the reward.

■ **But remember ...** As a rule of thumb, if your child has not got a good chance of earning the back-up reward at least twice a day, the system is unlikely to work. Older and more able youngsters *may* be able to cope with longer delays and with collecting their tokens for less frequent, but more elaborate, rewards. However, you do need to build towards this in gradual steps, rather than assume that they have the understanding, motivation and self-discipline from the very outset.

Case study

Leanne's parents had almost given up taking her shopping because of the tantrums she threw when she had had enough or could not have what she wanted. At 12 years old, she was too big to strap in a buggy and, once she had dropped to the ground, too heavy to be manhandled on to her feet. The only activity that really interested her was watching videos, so her parents decided to use this as an incentive. They prepared a small chart, showing outlines of four circles in a row, with a picture of a TV at the end of the row. To begin with, they went on very short shopping trips, visiting just one or two shops where problems were least likely. For every two or three minutes that went by with no tantrums, they put a sticker in one of the outlines, making sure that they reminded her that getting the sticker meant she could watch a video when she got home. They made sure that the last sticker was awarded close to the end of the trip, gave her the completed card to hold and let her exchange it for a video session as soon as she got home. They gradually extended the time she had to go without a tantrum before getting a sticker. The shopping expeditions were also made more demanding, visiting more shops in which she had no interest. If a tantrum did occur, her parents stood back until she calmed down, showed her the chart and said, 'See if you can get another sticker.' Stickers were never removed.

Case study

Stevie had developed the habit of frequently grabbing other people's clothing and hanging on for dear life. This tended to happen in the morning, during the more formal work session that led up to lunchtime. It seemed to have started as a way of avoiding demands, but Stevie now seemed to find it funny and appeared to enjoy the tussle that often resulted. Staff decided to take advantage of his very strong preference for pizza at lunchtime. They got a picture of a pizza and cut it into quarters, sticking the slices on to a matching outline using self-adhesive tabs of Velcro. To start with, Stevie did not have to do anything different, except learn to hand in the complete pizza when he made his choice at lunchtime. Once this routine was established, the outline was put on his table with one of the quarters missing, shortly before lunchtime. The work demands were fixed so that there was a good chance that Stevie would manage to complete five minutes of work without grabbing. When this happened, he was praised, staff gave him the missing slice to complete the outline and he immediately went to lunch where he could exchange the cut out pizza for the real thing. The amount of time that he had to go without grabbing was slowly extended to ten minutes. Then the outline was given earlier in the session, but this time with two slices missing. This process was repeated until he was starting with a blank outline. If ever he did grab, he was then expected to go for the set amount of time before he could get another slice. When he failed to complete the pizza, initially there was a serious tantrum, but staff persisted and he was only offered less favoured alternatives for lunch.

Robin was in his first year at secondary school and was having difficulties adjusting to the more formal ethos and the faster pace of work. Though not intentionally disruptive, he would often call out on impulse or fiddle with the belongings of the other youngsters on his table. The normal school report did not have any effect. Robin seemed to forget that he was being monitored and often could not understand why the teacher gave him a particular rating (whether good or bad). Things improved significantly when a new system was introduced. A daily report form was displayed on Robin's desk. For each lesson of the day, there was a row of ten small boxes containing ticks and a further row of ten blank boxes. At the top of the form, above the boxes with ticks, the two behaviours causing most concern were described (very briefly and specifically). Each time these occurred, the teacher would cancel one of the ticks. Above the blank boxes, two positive targets were identified – getting permission before calling out and getting on with his work. Although watching for positive behaviour was a lot harder for staff, they tried to award a tick in one of the empty boxes whenever they noticed Robin meeting the target. For each lesson, Robin could end up with a score of between 0 and 20 and his total for the day was linked with a small menu of rewards (some of which were provided by his parents at home). This system seemed to be much more meaningful and motivating for Robin. It provided a continual reminder of the targets and gave him a moment-by-moment picture of how he was doing – in any given lesson and in terms of the total for the day.

9

New results for old behaviour – changing the consequences of challenging behaviour

Introduction

Finally, we need to look at what can be done to change the pay-offs that the challenging behaviour seems to be achieving for your child. If the results of this behaviour can be altered, then it may be possible to reduce your child's motivation to behave in a given way. For practical purposes, it is useful to think in terms of three broad approaches:

- trying to stop the behaviour achieving its usual result – if your child no longer gets the pay-off, he may be less motivated to behave in that way
- imposing a cost by withdrawing something that your child enjoys whenever he engages in the behaviour
- punishing him by making something happen that we know he will find unpleasant – a strategy that clearly only differs in terms of degree from the previous point.

When you have to deal with challenging behaviour, a natural reaction is to start thinking in terms of deterrents – ways of discouraging your child from repeating the behaviour. We hope, having worked your way through the rest of the book, that you will appreciate the importance of considering all the other steps and strategies that we have outlined so far *before* focusing on changing the results of the behaviour. Particularly for children with autistic spectrum disorders, prevention is considerably better *and* easier than cure.

Changing the results of your child's behaviour may be a necessary and important part of your overall approach, but it is very unlikely to lead to long-term success if it is your only strategy. As we explained at the start of Chapter 7, focusing on what you want your child to *stop* doing is only half the story. In the longer term, you can only prevent challenging behaviour if you also help your child to develop skills and behaviour that let him achieve the same (or equivalent) results or that serve the same purpose but in a more effective and acceptable way. If you only focus on efforts to discourage the problem behaviour, you are not helping your child to understand or learn what you *do* want him to do. Just as importantly, you are not helping him to learn different and better ways to achieve the same results. Any plan for tackling challenging behaviour needs, first and foremost, to include prevention and contain strategies for teaching and encouraging new skills and behaviours.

Reducing the pay-off

The first five steps of the Plan should have helped you identify the results and pay-offs that are motivating your child's behaviour. At the moment, this behaviour is probably the quickest and easiest way for your child to achieve these results. To begin with, any new skills and behaviours are likely to involve your child in more effort (compared with simply following old patterns). Therefore, new rewards and pay-offs will not seem as attractive as the old favourites. For this reason, we need to find ways of reducing the motivation that keeps the old behaviour going. Eliminating – or at least reducing – the pay-off is the first strategy to try.

Before proceeding further, it is important to sound a note of caution. If you are dealing with a well-established behaviour, your child will have had lots of time and opportunity to learn the links between what he does and the results this achieves. If you do succeed in blocking or reducing the pay-off, his first reaction is likely to be one of doing the same, but more of it. This is probably how most of us would behave in a similar situation – a little bit of the old behaviour seems not to be working any longer, so maybe a lot of it will! For people with autistic spectrum disorders, switching off old behaviour and shifting to a new pattern can be especially difficult. This is one form of the more general problem of lack of flexibility of thinking and behaviour. What this means in practice is that the problem may well get worse before it gets better.

There are a number of ways in which you can try to reduce the pay-off that your child is getting from his behaviour.

- **Alter the environment** This may help to reduce the impact of the behaviour. In turn, it may also reduce the pay-off your child gets. This applies especially when your child seems to be motivated by the sensory effects of his behaviour. To take an extreme example, if all glass is toughened, then your child will not get the enjoyment of seeing and hearing the window shatter. If toys and objects in the environment are not breakable or (as was the case with one child) secured on short lengths of cord, so they can be used but not thrown, then the motivation to throw may gradually decline.

Case study

Rory discovered the 'pleasures' of tearing down his bedroom curtains during a particularly prolonged outburst when he lost his temper. He soon began to experiment to find out how hard he had to tug to pull them down again. He obviously enjoyed the impact of his behaviour. He was also quick to recognise the upset that he caused and seemed quite entertained by his parents' efforts to refit the curtain track and sort out the curtains. His parents finally hit on the idea of using Velcro to fix the curtains to the heading tape. Rory could still pull them down, but he lost most of the physical and sensory rewards that were motivating this behaviour. Because he was not doing any real damage and it was so easy to refit the curtains, his parents found it much easier to control their own reactions, too. This meant that Rory was no longer getting the additional reward that their responses seemed to have been providing.

■ **Reassurance for you** As the previous example illustrates, another important reason for altering the environment is to help you. If you feel reasonably confident that your child cannot do too much harm to himself or the things around him, then you may find it easier to respond in a low-key manner.

Case study

David had got into the habit of only settling to sleep if one of his parents lay on the bed beside him – a process that could take up to two hours. This pattern had developed because of David's reluctance to go to bed or stay in his room when left. His parents finally realised that there was no way in which they could actually control when David went to sleep, but they could try to prevent him constantly leaving his bedroom and disturbing everyone else in the house. They set up a predictable, calming bedtime routine, made sure he had toys and a favourite tape and installed a form of stairgate so that he was unable to get out (but could have the reassurance of the door being ajar). Even though his parents did everything they could to make being in his bedroom as pleasant as possible, they still felt uneasy about leaving him on his own before he was asleep. They dealt with their main concerns in two ways. They covered most of the floor with thick rugs and dressed David in a warm sleepsuit, so that it did not matter if he fell asleep while playing on the floor. In addition, because David had a bit of a fascination with lightbulbs, they installed a downlighter, recessed into the ceiling, which could be controlled with a dimmer switch. Although there was little real chance of David coming to any harm, these arrangements gave his parents the confidence to persist and put up with his initial protests about being left in his room. They did consider following the common tip of making regular, brief checks to see how he was, but decided that this might keep him awake, given that he was quite a sociable youngster who was good at getting others to interact with him.

■ **Keeping reactions low key** Other people's reactions can be a part (and sometimes the most interesting part!) of the results that challenging behaviour produces. Your child may be seeking attention or may just enjoy the excitement or sense of having made something happen. Even if these types of pay-off are not currently motivating your child, it is sensible to avoid the risk of them becoming an influence. Exactly what 'low key' means for you and your child will depend on the behaviour and situation. It could mean completely ignoring the behaviour or getting on with clearing up as quickly and quietly as possible. Another aspect of a low-key reaction is the language you use. If you are not going to totally ignore the behaviour, remember to keep your language simple, keep the tone neutral and try to be as clear as possible about what you do want.

Case study

By the time she was six, Amber had discovered that grabbing adults' hair and weaving her fingers into it was a highly effective way of establishing a sort of interaction and creating a stir. She never seemed to do this in anger – she would often be smiling and seemed to genuinely enjoy the coaxing and physical contact that resulted. It usually happened when people were working with or talking to her. Amber's parents and teachers had set themselves the medium-term target of teaching her other ways to make contact, gain attention and play with people. In the short term, though, they needed an effective way to reduce Amber's motivation to grab hair. They decided that whenever she did this, they would try to immobilise her hand by trapping it under their own hand against their heads. This was quite effective in preventing Amber from actually pulling their hair and allowed them to continue what they were doing or simply wait. Though it sometimes took a few minutes, Amber usually ended up releasing her grip, which was considerably less painful than trying to disentangle her fingers.

- **Dealing with the after-effects** This is another part of keeping reactions low key, and is especially important if your child enjoys the impact that his behaviour creates. At the most basic level, this may mean wiping up the spit or removing the remains of the broken plate so that any sensory reward is quickly neutralised. If your child has hurt someone, the victim needs to be given whatever comfort is required, but preferably out of the child's sight. Alterations to the environment can obviously be helpful when dealing with the after-effects – wipe-clean surfaces help to reduce the impact and stress of all sorts of smearing or scribbling, for example.

- **Withholding rewards** Some challenging behaviour is very clearly a means of achieving a specific reward. Your child may have forced you into the trap of providing a chocolate bar to head off a tantrum at the supermarket checkout. Even if he does not know how to communicate, he may have learned that if he bangs and shouts when he is feeling thirsty, someone will come and eventually think about offering him a drink. He may have realised that he is allowed to go to the head of the dinnertime queue if he argues with those in front of him. Your child is likely to persist in these ways of behaving unless you are able to find some way of withholding the rewards that motivate him to do these things (the advice in Chapter 5 may help you to deal with his reactions when you do this). Where a child seems to be motivated by sensations that are actually part of the behaviour – screaming, spinning or hand flapping, for example – it is considerably harder to withhold the pay-off or reward.

- **Dealing with avoidance** Challenging behaviour is sometimes used as a means of avoiding or escaping from a demand. Your child learns that if he puts up enough resistance, he will not be asked to go into a lesson or made to switch off the video. Dealing with this sort of situation can be very tricky. Making a particular demand on your child may feel like it is more trouble than it is worth. If you do decide that the battle is worth fighting and that your child really is able to cope with the demand that you are placing on him, then you need to prepare for it. You will need time, energy, an environment that helps to minimise any damage – and lots of rewards for any positive behaviour.

The need for consistency

Whatever way you decide to go about reducing the pay-off, you will need to stick at your chosen strategy. You need to get your child past the stage where he thinks (or hopes!) that the old behaviour will do the trick. You also need to be aware that, once a pattern of behaviour has become established, it only needs occasional rewards to keep it going. In actual fact, occasional, unpredictable rewards may well have the effect of strengthening the behaviour. What they teach your child is that he will get the reward or pay-off – he just needs to persist.

Ignoring behaviour – some guidelines

This is one of the pieces of advice that you are most likely to be offered. It is one of the easiest to give, but possibly the hardest to put into practice. In the right circumstances, it can be very effective. However, you do need to be sure that it fits the problem and plan its implementation carefully. The following guidelines may help.

- **What problems are best dealt with by ignoring?** Ignoring is best used for those sorts of behaviour that are aimed at getting attention or that are rewarded by something in the adult's reaction to it. As we pointed out in Chapter 7, this sort of motivation may actually be less common in children with autistic spectrum disorders than in other children. Before considering the use of ignoring the behaviour as a strategy, you need to think carefully about what is motivating it. If the behaviour may actually be an expression of feeling – a reaction to pain or anxiety, for instance – then it must not be ignored.

- **Is it safe to ignore the behaviour?** Ignoring should not be used for behaviour that is, or could be, dangerous to your child or others around him. It may be possible to modify the environment in such a way that the risk can be reduced to an acceptable level.

- **Can you manage to ignore it – and what about others?** Even if there is no risk to the child or to other people, you need to decide whether or not you will be able to ignore it. You need to take into account any disruption that your child will cause – something that is clearly a crucial issue in schools. You also need to think about your own tolerance levels. We all differ in terms of the behaviours that get to us or the degree of noise, mess or disruption to routine that we can put up with. You also need to think about how other people will react and what *their* tolerance levels are.

- **Sharing the plan** Try to ensure that everyone else understands and accepts the plan. Make sure, too, that they know it will get worse before it gets better.

- **Plan your own reactions** Decide what you are going to do while ignoring your child. At the very least, ensure that you are looking away and remaining as expressionless as you can. Deliberately and obviously doing something else may help make the point. It may also help to reduce your own frustration and any temptation to react.

- **Keep track of progress** Any change is likely to be slow and gradual, so it may be helpful to keep a record of the frequency of the behaviour you are focusing on. After the early phase where things are likely to get worse, the record should then show a gradual improvement. This may help give you the determination and confidence to carry on

- **Ensure you have support** Because any change is likely to be gradual and it is actually very hard to do nothing, try at least to get some moral support while you carry through this strategy.

- **Reward positive behaviour** This can be extremely hard to do if you have just had to stand by, watching your child disrupting the classroom or kicking and thrashing outside the supermarket. The moment any acceptable behaviour does occur, however, you need to step in with some form of reward or encouragement. This is the only way to get across the vital message about what behaviour *will* result in the attention that your child seeks.

Case study

There had always been occasional instances of David slapping his head or regurgitating his food. By the time he was ten, he had become much more interested in interacting with others, but seemed to be using the slapping and regurgitation as a way of gaining attention. Daily one-to-one interaction sessions were set up, with the aim of teaching David action rhymes and other routines. It was hoped that he could use these as a way of establishing and maintaining interaction. These were very lively sessions and involved a lot of imitation. Whenever the problem behaviour occurred, the adult working with him would immediately stop what she was doing and go limp – head down, face expressionless, shoulders and arms drooping. Only when David stopped the behaviour would she spring back to life. Once he seemed to understand this connection (and clearly preferred the lively version of the adult) the same strategy was used in the classroom. This seemed to work reasonably well, provided members of staff were able to respond whenever David used his new, acceptable strategies to gain attention and they made a point of interacting with him every so often.

Case study

The reactions of classmates can often be a significant factor in motivating some types of challenging behaviour, particularly with older children who have higher levels of understanding. By his first year of secondary school, Andrew had learned that a well-timed swear word could liven up a lesson and earn him a certain amount of status among his classmates. Staff dealt with it in two ways. After a lengthy discussion with the class about what was going on, the children were offered incentives – both for not responding when the swearing occurred *and* for any overall reduction in Andrew's swearing. This made sure that the class did not have a vested interest in the swearing continuing and gave Andrew the chance to do something positive for his classmates. To avoid resentment that Andrew was getting away with it, this was also linked with the school's usual system of sanctions. After three warnings, Andrew was briefly removed from the lesson, and if this happened three times in a day, he was put on supervised lunch.

Imposing a cost

By 'imposing a cost' we mean withdrawing something that your child enjoys as a direct and immediate consequence of that specific problem behaviour. Ideally, this is about making sure that your child experiences what might be considered the natural consequences of his behaviour. A toy is thrown, so he loses the opportunity to play with it for the next five minutes. He shouts while watching the TV, so it is turned off. He messes about in class, so he has to complete the work in his own time. Where there is not an obvious natural consequence, you can try imposing a cost by taking away or withholding something that you know your child likes.

This is a fairly common strategy in the classroom or home, regardless of whether or not a child has some type of special need. It can be more difficult to use effectively with children with autistic spectrum disorders, for all the same reasons that it may be difficult to use rewards effectively. It may be hard to actually identify a treat or privilege that you can withdraw or that will make any difference to your child. Even if you can, he will not always understand the link between his actions and the cost that you impose. Sometimes withdrawing a treat may also trigger a serious tantrum, so that the 'solution' actually makes matters worse.

Before you set about using this strategy, it is worth stating (or restating) a few general principles. For the most part, these are very similar to the guidelines given for using rewards effectively offered in the last chapter.

- **Your child must have something to lose** If he has no positive experiences, treats or privileges, then you cannot take anything away from him. For this reason, it is especially important that you are actively rewarding and encouraging other sorts of positive behaviour. Above, we gave the example of David and stressed that the approach only worked in the classroom when staff made a conscious effort to interact with him. This helped to emphasise the contrast between the limp reaction whenever he did head-slap or regurgitate and the attention and fun that was available at other times.

- **Choose a specific target** You cannot deal with all the problems at once, and this approach works best if you focus on a single, specific one. Doing so helps your child to make a clear link. Try to avoid very broad and vague targets, such as 'being bad'.

- **Immediate and consistent** The cost needs to be something that you can impose immediately and consistently after each occurrence of the behaviour. If the consequence is too remote from the actual behaviour, your child is unlikely to be able to make the connection (unless he has quite a sophisticated level of understanding). Even if your child is able to understand that he is going to miss his trip to the swimming pool next week, you can only take this away from him once.

- **Little and often** It is also important that the cost is something that you are prepared to impose consistently on a little and often basis. Do not threaten something that you end up feeling guilty about – this is likely to undermine your efforts to be consistent.

- **Get the message across** Use language that is as simple as possible to link the behaviour and the cost: 'No throwing – car away', for example. You may also want to use a picture or illustration to reinforce the message.

- **Give him a way back** As soon as you have imposed a cost, try to find or create the earliest possible opportunity to reward and encourage your child. He needs to have a way of regaining whatever you have taken away from him.

Case study

Samantha had an overwhelming interest in the computer and her teacher was trying to turn this into a more social form of activity. She paired Samantha with another child and used a program that required them to take turns. The other youngster was not as proficient as Samantha, so every so often Samantha would lose patience and try to take over. Whenever this happened, her teacher would immediately move her off the computer and put her on the 'thinking chair' for three minutes. In the end, her desire to be on the computer overcame her reluctance and frustration about sharing.

Case study

In the last chapter, we described Robin's token system. This allowed an immediate, but low-key response to the two priority problems. Because he was also able to earn ticks, this gave him a way of earning his way back to a reward. The fact that there were also different levels of reward and that his score could be carried over to the next day all reduced the likelihood of him giving up in frustration.

Case study

Lee was a very able 14-year-old attending a mainstream school. He was deliberately withdrawn from some lessons to help keep his stress levels down and his classmates were actively encouraged to support him. Difficulties began to develop when it was time for him to return to his normal lessons. Lee would storm about, shouting angrily, often emptying shelves and turning over furniture in the withdrawal room where he was taught. Staff members were very conscious of the difficulties he experienced and tried to keep the demands on Lee to manageable levels. They felt his behaviour was a quite calculated attempt to get his own way. They also feared that spending even more time out of lessons would actually make matters worse. Lee would lose his links with his classmates and could easily talk himself into a worse state of worry about what might happen on his return to lessons. They arranged for a couple of classmates to call at the room and walk with Lee to his lessons. If Lee refused to go, then (with his parents' agreement) he was made to catch up on any work that was missed, either at break or lunchtime. Any mess that he had created in the withdrawal room had to be cleared up and the whole room set to rights – in Lee's own time, after school.

Using time out

You may have tried this already, even if you did not call it by this name, or the strategy may have been recommended to you. Time out tends to be one of the more commonly used approaches. In the home, it usually means removing your child from the situation for a set period of time – sending him into the hall, bedroom or some other place with as few distractions and sources of entertainment as possible. In school, your child may be removed to another part of the classroom or sent to a withdrawal room or office.

Time out is not intended to be a punishment in the strict sense. The aim is to remove your child from any possible sources of reward in the situation that may be encouraging or maintaining the behaviour. It is essential to emphasize that this should not be a matter of sending him to somewhere that is intentionally unpleasant.

The term 'time out' also tends to be used to refer to the practice of taking your child out of a situation so that he has an opportunity to calm down. This can help, by lowering the level of stimulation or removing demands that may have been triggering the problem. Your child may well gain reassurance from the fact that an adult is willing and able to step in and take charge of the situation. In effect, the adult is offering 'sanctuary' and this may be a better description than 'time out'. However, even when the adult is intending to use time out in the strict sense, as described above, it may well offer an element of sanctuary to him.

Before considering using time out, you need to think and plan carefully, taking the following guidelines into account.

- Time out may be effective if your child's behaviour is motivated by the reactions of others or the impact that his behaviour is having on the immediate environment.
- Do *not* use time out if your child seems intent on avoiding demands or actively tries to avoid social interaction. Being on their own may actually reward some children with autistic spectrum disorders.
- Do *not* use this approach if your child is likely to engage in dangerous behaviour while spending time out.

- Choose a place for time out that allows you to keep an eye on your child. Avoid anywhere that will provide him with pleasant distractions. You do not always have to remove him from the room – you might need to do no more than turn his chair away from the table or sit him in the corner.
- Time out will only work if you are able to use it consistently and immediately as a response to specific behaviours that you want to target, rather than as a blanket reaction to 'being bad'. You need to make sure that other adults in your child's environment know about the arrangement and are willing and able to support it.
- The period of time spent in time out should be brief – ideally in the range of two to five minutes. Any longer than this and your child may well find ways to entertain himself, the danger then being that the time out becomes a welcome break. On the other hand, some children may become anxious or agitated by prolonged periods without direct attention, triggering other forms of challenging behaviour.
- Keep a track of how often you use time out and for how long. If you find that you are relying on it more and more, then it clearly is not working – it may even be counterproductive.
- When you move your child into time out, try to do it in as low key a way as you can manage. Make sure that you spell out what he has done and the consequence.
- Bring your child out of time out after the interval that you have specified. If your child is still behaving inappropriately at this point, extend the time out until there is at least a brief lull. If you fail to do this, then you may be accidentally teaching your child that he just needs to persist with the problem behaviour in order to get out.
- Find (or invent) the first possible opportunity for praising, rewarding or paying attention to your child.

If your child will stay in the designated place, it is worth persisting for a while. You may even need to physically prompt him to return, while providing him with the least possible attention as you do so. If this does not work, then you may have to abandon time out as some children come to enjoy the element of chase that may develop.

Case study

Tony developed the habit of grabbing other youngsters in his class, mainly because he seemed to enjoy seeing them being upset by it and the excitement he created. As many of these children were very frail, members of staff were concerned and had no choice but to intervene very quickly. Time out on a chair in the corridor had been tried, but Tony would bang on the door and seemed to quite like watching passers-by. His teacher decided to make use of the partially covered courtyard that could be reached directly from her classroom. Net curtains were hung so that Tony at least couldn't see the reaction that his banging on the window created. Because it was winter, staff felt it necessary to get Tony into his coat before putting him outside. To reduce the delay that this caused, it was hung on the handle of the door that led to the courtyard. Quite quickly, Tony began to respond to the time out. Quite by accident, staff realised that the sight of his coat hung on the door handle was actually working as a deterrent. It seemed to remind Tony of the rules. If he seemed to be building up to grabbing, it was sometimes enough just to draw his attention to the coat.

Making something unpleasant happen – punishment

Many of the techniques already mentioned in this chapter could be described as forms of punishment. However, there is an important difference between these approaches and deliberately use of pain or inflicting some other unpleasant experience on your child in order to deter challenging behaviour. Among professionals, the climate of opinion regarding these latter methods changed significantly in the 1980s and 1990s. Members of staff in schools are now specifically forbidden to use punishments that involve deliberately inflicting pain. Across all groups of professionals there is probably almost total agreement that it is preferable to use the sort of preventive and positive methods described in previous chapters.

However, debate continues as to whether or not there may be some exceptional circumstances in which it is justifiable to deliberately use unpleasant experiences (or 'aversives' as they are often termed). Usually, people are referring to the sort of challenging behaviour that could seriously threaten the child's physical well-being or might result in a very serious restriction of the child's opportunities and life experiences. Even those who do advocate the use of these approaches would also accept the importance of preventive measures and ensuring that alternative skills are taught and encouraged.

In the United Kingdom, parents have discretion about the methods they use to manage their children's behaviour. Everyone will be aware, however, that the climate of opinion is changing. There has been a steady shift in what is considered acceptable, although no precise legal definitions and limits exist. Just like all parents, the parents of children with autistic spectrum disorders need to decide where they stand on this issue, taking into account their own values, the nature of their child's difficulties, level of understanding and the challenging behaviour they are faced with.

In coming to a view, we think that it is important to consider the following issues.

- Many of the problem behaviours presented by children with autistic spectrum disorders are a reaction to anxiety or are due to a lack of coping or communication skills. In such circumstances, it would be reasonable to say that your child does not know any other way to behave and so we would question the fairness of using aversive methods to try and change the behaviour. Certainly most parents would want to weigh up whether or not they thought their child had behaved in a particular way 'on purpose' and if he actually had the understanding and skills to behave differently.
- Some of the behaviour of children with autistic spectrum disorders has a compulsive element – this applies particularly to rituals and certain sorts of repetitive behaviour. Your child may experience an overpowering urge to repeat the particular routine or pattern of behaviour. Quite literally, it may be beyond his control. Again, we would argue that it might not be reasonable to use punishments in such circumstances. Often these patterns of behaviour seem to be a reaction to, or even a method of coping with, anxiety. The fear of punishment may actually make it more likely that your child will engage in the very behaviour that it is intended to deter.
- Problems with seeing things from other people's points of view and being sensitive to their feelings and well-being are core difficulties in autism. This lack of concern for others can be very distressing. It can also be very frustrating for adults because with

normally developing children this can be one of the main motivations to behave in an acceptable way. Over time, it is sometimes possible to encourage the development of higher levels of empathy. However, it is important to emphasise that, for many youngsters, this lack of awareness and concern for others is part of the disability. It is not something that your child can directly help or do anything about.

■ Aversive methods, like most forms of punishment, do little or nothing to teach your child how to behave. They may motivate him to avoid the person who punishes or to avoid detection, but do nothing directly to help your child develop the necessary coping skills or learn acceptable behaviours.

■ The instinct to punish is a very common and understandable reaction – particularly when we are under stress and if we have been hurt or feel threatened. Most people will also recognise that this instinct often has more to do with making ourselves feel better than helping your child to behave differently. Sometimes this also results in an immediate, though short-term, improvement in your child's behaviour. This may encourage the use of this sort of punishment again, and it is quite easy to become reliant on it – often with a gradual increase in its frequency or intensity.

In our experience, most parents faced with seriously challenging behaviour have been tempted, from time to time, to use some sort of physical punishment. In our experience, it is relatively rare for this to have the long-term effect that the adult is looking for. However, very many parents will have given in to the temptation or have reached a conscious decision at least to try a smack. There may be times when you feel that you have been left with little alternative. If you do find yourself in this situation, it is important to bear in mind the advice given at the end of Chapter 2 about looking after yourself.

Being responsible for a child who presents challenging behaviour is tremendously stressful. In the heat of the moment, your actions will not always be as rational as you would like and your own needs may seem every bit as important as your child's. Remember that it is never too late to go back to the drawing board and think things through in terms of the Eight-step Plan. We hope that the advice we have offered does provide you with real alternatives to punishment.

Further reading

Clements, John, and Zarkowska, Eva (1992) *Problem Behaviour in People with Severe Learning Disabilities: A practical guide to a constructional approach*. London: Chapman & Hall.

Gray, Carol (1995) 'Teaching children with autism to read social situations' in K. A. Quill (ed.), *Teaching Children with Autism*. New York: Delmar Publishers.

Happé, Francesca (1994) *Autism: An introduction to psychological theory*. London: UCL Press.

Hewett, Dave (ed.) (1998) *Challenging Behaviour: Principles and practices*. London: David Fulton Publishers.

Howlin, Patricia (1998) *Children with Autism and Asperger Syndrome: A guide for practitioners and parents*. Chichester: John Wiley.

Jordan, Rita, and Jones, Glenys (1999) *Meeting the Needs of Children with Autistic Spectrum Disorders*. London: David Fulton Publishers.

Leicester City Council and Leicestershire County Council (1998) *Asperger Syndrome: Practical strategies for the classroom: a teacher's guide*. London: The National Autistic Society.

Leicestershire County Council and Fosse Health Trust (1998) *Autism: How to help your young child*. London: The National Autistic Society.

Schopler, Eric (ed.) (1995) *Parent Survival Manual*. New York: Plenum Press.

Schopler, Eric, Mesibov, Gary, and Hearsey, Kathy (1995) 'Structured teaching in the TEACCH system', Chapter 13 in Eric Schopler and Gary Mesibov (eds), *Learning and Cognition in Autism*. New York: Plenum Press.

Wheeler, Maria (1998) *Toilet Training for Individuals with Autism and Related Disorders: a Comprehensive Guide for Parents and Teachers*. Arlington, Texas: Future Horizons Inc.

Wing, Lorna (1996) *The Autistic Spectrum: A guide for parents and professionals*. London: Constable.

Index of problems

This index lists all the problem behaviours that are mentioned or discussed in the book. It will help you to quickly find out how other people have tackled a specific problem that may be causing you concern. It is a selection from the main index, where other topics can be found.

Index

Index by David Potter

John Clement
'People with autism
behaving badly.'